Bulletproof Vests vs. the Ethic of Care

Which Strategy Is Your School Using?

Edited by
Denise Smith

A SCARECROWEDUCATION BOOK

The Scarecrow Press, Inc.
Lanham, Maryland, and Oxford
2003

A SCARECROWEDUCATION BOOK

Published in the United States of America
by Scarecrow Press, Inc.
A Member of the Rowman & Littlefield Publishing Group
4501 Forbes Boulevard, Suite 200, Lanham, Maryland 20706
www.scarecroweducation.com

PO Box 317
Oxford
OX2 9RU, UK

British Library Cataloguing in Publication Information Available

Library of Congress Cataloging-in-Publication Data

Bulletproof vests vs. the ethic of care : which strategy is your school
using? / [edited by] Denise Smith.
  p. cm.
"A ScarecrowEducation book."
Includes bibliographical references and index.
 ISBN 0-8108-4618-7 (pbk. : alk. paper)
 1. School violence—United States—Prevention. 2. Conflict management—
Study and teaching—United States. I. Title: Bulletproof vests versus the ethic
of care. II. Smith, Denise, 1965–
LB3013.32 .S65 2003
371.7'82'0973—dc21

                 2002015492

Contents

In loving memory of Jamie Skarbek
and any child in America who has been a victim or
witness of violence

Figures and Tables

FIGURES

TABLES

Foreword

Denise Smith and her colleagues have addressed one of the most disturbing social problems facing the nation at the beginning of the twenty-first century: school violence. The tragic drama of school violence played out in the 1990s brought terror to the hearts of parents whose children were in school and stark tragedy to the families whose children were involved in the violent acts committed in schools.

Emphasis in this book is on school violence, not youth violence, and it offers a positive perspective in interpreting available data and opening the conversation about opportunities for positive interventions. The authors make three major observations that clearly lean in the direction of hope for public schools. First, research suggests that schools are among the safest places for children and adolescents. Most serious acts of violence happen outside of school.

Second, notwithstanding portrayals in the public media, data now suggest that violence in schools is not increasing and is, in fact, decreasing in some areas. James Hurst and John King remind the reader, however, that available research lacks the clarity of consistent definitions, rigor, and scope needed to proffer more specific conclusions. Third, school violence is complex, with students and the schools they attend being part of a larger social ecology made up of families and communities. Hurst, King, and Smith point out that, although individuals, families, peer groups, communities, and schools have risk factors, the cause of school violence cannot be established clearly as associated with either one. There are, however, clear correlates with gangs and substance abuse, for example.

A long line of sociological research has pointed to social contexts having more power in accounting for variance in behavior than the characteristics of individuals. This is born out by the U.S. Secret Service report cited by Smith that there is "no useful 'profile' of students engaged in targeted school violence." In other words, individual student characteristics do not account for the variance in explaining violent acts in school.

Some have raised the possibility that children with disabilities contribute disproportionately to the problems of school violence. Smith, examining this issue, pointed out that none of the school-yard shooters have been students identified as having disabilities. However, some children with disabilities, especially some of those identified as having emotional disabilities, may be at risk for committing violent acts. This is a difficult area to sort through because of the problems of definition and the many variables involved in any specific action. What is clear, however, is the fact that, as pointed out in the Secret Service study, some of the children committing violent acts have been those having difficulty coping with loss, personal failure, and bullies. They have been those experiencing themselves in the world as victims of persecution and some have been suicidal.

One of the major challenges in coming to terms with the nature of school violence and understanding it in ways that can lead to preventive interventions has been the limitations of theory. Patricia A. Parrish, in this volume, suggests Bronfenbrenner's ecological theory of human development and Noddings's theory of an ethic of care as being two complementary conceptions of social behavior that can be useful in understanding the needs and the work to be done. These theories make explicit the complex interactions that account for behavior and the power of human relationships. They have clear implications for school policy, teacher education, and research aimed at making schools safer and improving students' experience of safety.

Smith, Parrish, and Karen B. Clark, in the last three chapters, explore these implications for preventing violence in schools, families, and communities. Their analyses are guided by Bronfenbrenner's and Noddings's ecological and care models, respectively. These three chapters are rich in examining the research literature and focusing on targeted interventions in schools, homes, and communities.

The media put faces on school violence and, perhaps unwittingly, reinforce the idea that school violence is about the volitional acts of individuals. While individuals perpetrate violent acts, the faces of systems that coax, model, reinforce, fail to nurture, and otherwise participate in the individual motivations for violent actions are more difficult to describe. We are accustomed to thinking about specific causes such as gravity that causes an unsupported object to fall to the ground or friction that causes heat.

We think about cause in the social world as blame for actions. For example, someone must be blamed for a student's violent action. The usual suspects are the unruly child, gang influence, bad parents, or uncaring teachers. None of these usual suspects appears to be complicit in the violent acts in schools in the 1990s. We are less accustomed to thinking about human behavior as a product of many things working together, some of which promote healthy attitudes and actions and some of which do not. The two theories offered in this book—social ecology of human behavior and an ethic of care—provide useful leverage in opening up a view of the complex social contexts in which school violence occurs.

The current political slogan, "Leave no child behind" is interesting in its implications. It does not say, "No child should fall behind." Rather, it implicitly calls for advocacy and change in the systems charged with responsibility for enabling children to keep up. It carries both academic and social meanings and suggests an ethic of inclusion and care.

Safety in a democracy is difficult, as the terrorist attack of September 11, 2001, clearly indicates. Actions that increase safety tend to decrease freedom. The trade-off of freedoms for safety, neither of which is ever absolute, is a major public policy issue. A similar issue exists in school policy. Schools are places where this balance can be most precarious. Somewhere between relatively unrestrained freedom and lockdown, school policies have to make sense in creating and sustaining safe learning environments for students and teachers. Hallways in schools are social analogs to streets in cities, with all of the social rewards of connecting with friends and the risks of harm in crowds with relative strangers.

School violence also created major challenges for school leaders with responsibility for school policies. Liberal education policies were challenged and some schools moved close to the brink of lockdown. In addition to being beleaguered by attacks on the quality of teachers and on educational outcomes of students since the early 1980s, leaders now face the reality that schools are not safe or, more accurately, are not experienced as safe. Further, a study sponsored by the Metropolitan Life

Insurance Company found that 39 percent of students they interviewed do not trust their teachers.

One of the clear themes in this book is the importance of emotional as well as physical safety of students. What students believe about their welfare in school, that is, their safety, affects their learning and behavior. The ethic of care certainly offers a focus on the emotional qualities of the relationships between students and their teachers. Likewise, the social ecology of behavior keeps the focus on the roles of different social systems in the nurture of children.

Smith and her colleagues have provided a clear picture of research on the nature of school violence and a useful theoretical framework within which to understand the issues. They neither oversimplify the problems nor do they present them as beyond the scope of reasonable interventions. Rather, they offer empirically validated and sensible guidance for interventions in schools, families, and communities.

Peter Senge tells the story of a greeting among the tribes of northern Natal in South Africa. *Sawu bona,* the English equivalent of "hello," literally means "I see you." One of the challenges to care for children, and to provide the kind of safety they need to experience in school and elsewhere, is to be able to see them and, in seeing them, to be able to appreciate the kinds of the social, psychological, moral, and economic forces that impact and shape their lives. "Good morning, students" should be more than a cultural habit, individual differences more than an academic slogan, and rigor in research more than a commitment to designs that fail to capture the complexity of children's lives. School violence is not a euphemism for bad kids doing bad things in school. It is a cluster of social problems centered in the lives children bring to schools. Smith and her colleagues provide a useful, and hopeful, analysis of these challenges.

—James L. Paul, professor, University of South Florida

Preface

YOUTH VIOLENCE

Overall, the statistics on youth and school violence do not provide evidence to support extreme levels of concern from either the media or public. With regard to juvenile crime, arrest rates, documented in Snyder (2002), support the trend toward an overall decrease in juvenile crime since the mid-1990s and include the following:

- Juvenile murder arrests have steadily declined since 1993 with the number of arrests in 2000 (1,200) less than one-third that of 1993.
- Juvenile arrests for burglary have declined substantially since 1980.
- The rate of juvenile arrests for Violent Crime Index offenses (murder, forcible rape, robbery, and aggravated assault) in 2000 have declined for the sixth consecutive year.
- The percentage of overall violent crimes from 1994 to 2000 attributed to juveniles dropped 41 percent to a level of 309 arrests for every 100,000 ages 10–17.
- The juvenile arrest rate for Property Crime Index offenses in 2000 was at its lowest level since at least 1980.

We can also see a decrease in the prevalence of violent behavior within and related to the school setting. Kaufman et al. (2001) cite the following information:

- In general, students experience significantly less serious violent crime at school than away from school.
- There was a general decline in violent victimization rates both at school and away from school from 1993 to 1999.
- The percentage of students who reported being in a fight away from school declined from 42 percent to 36 percent from 1993 to 1999.
- The percentage of students who reported being in a fight away from school declined slightly from 1993 to 1999 (16 percent to 14 percent).
- The percentage of students who reported carrying a weapon anywhere fell from 22 percent to 17 percent between the years of 1993 and 1999.

Although these statistics show a decline in youth crime and youth and school violence, there are other statistics that show a less clear picture of overall youth behavior and school safety. Some survey data paints quite a different picture of decrease in youth violence (U.S. Surgeon General 2001). Substance use and weapon availability are major risk factors for youth violence.

The information reported based on self-report and governmental data shows either an increase or no significant change concerning juvenile crime and arrests which either directly or indirectly affect school violence and safety:

- Trends in juvenile arrest rates for weapons law violations and for murder were similar between 1980 and 2000 (Snyder 2002).
- Between 1993 and 1999, the percentage of students in grades 9 through 12 who were threatened or injured with a weapon on school property in the previous twelve months remained constant: 7 percent to 8 percent (Kaufman et al. 2001).
- Between 1990 and 2000, arrests of juveniles for drug abuse violations increased 145 percent (Snyder 2002).
- From 1993 to 1999, there was an increase from 24 percent to 32 percent of students who reported the availability of illegal drugs on school property (Kaufman et al. 2001).
- The percentage of students that report consuming alcohol from 1993 to 1999 remained unchanged. This is for consumption on and away from school property (Kaufman et al. 2001).

- Self-report data show no decrease and, in fact, show an increase from 1993 to 1998 for serious violence among 12th graders (U.S. Surgeon General 2001).
- Around 3 out of 10 high school seniors have reported committing a violent act in the past year. This 30 percent rate has not changed in the last twenty years (Johnston 2000).
- Only 6 percent to 14 percent of chronic violent offenders are ever arrested for serious violent crime (U.S. Surgeon General 2001).
- Despite an increase in the percentage of students and teachers who feel safe at school (Kaufman et al. 2001), 25 percent to 30 percent of public school students, teachers, and law enforcement officials think that violence in their school will increase in the future.

Overall, the data point to a decline in youth violence and school violence during the past six to eight years. Compared with the high rate of youth violence that occurred from 1983 to 1994, more recent years have shown clear decreases in arrest rates for violent crimes.

However, some estimates of youth violence activity based on data other than arrest rates, that is, confidential self-reports, and the prevalence of major risk factors, do not show the decreases seen with arrest rates. While there clearly is good news with many indicators evidencing decreased violence, law enforcement or school officials continue to document cause for concern in some indicators, which may not be easily observed.

OVERVIEW OF BOOK

For the purpose of this book, *school violence* is defined as any act or threat of physical or verbal force with the intent to inflict pain or harm the well-being of another person (Rudo, Robbins, and Smith 2002). The first chapter, as mentioned earlier, provides an overview of school and youth violence and is followed by a chapter on the risk factors for violence. The third chapter addresses concerns about children with special needs and their involvement with violence. The fourth chapter begins with an overview of Bronfenbrenner's and Noddings's theories and then provides a connection between them. This is critical to understanding the prevention/intervention strategies described in the final three chapters. The fifth chapter focuses on prevention and intervention strategies reviewed and recommended by the U.S. Surgeon General and how these interventions/preventions strategies reflect the theoretical framework of Noddings and Bronfenbrenner, and is followed by a chapter on families and effective prevention/intervention techniques. Chapter 7 examines community violence prevention and intervention techniques as reviewed by the U.S. Surgeon General and supported by the theories espoused by Noddings and Bronfenbrenner.

REFERENCES

Johnston, L. D. 2000. *Monitoring the future survey: National results on adolescent drug use*. Washington, D.C.: U.S. Department of Health and Human Services, National Institute of Health, at monitoringthefuture.org (accessed March 14, 2002).

Kaufman, P., X. Chen, S. P. Choy, K. Peter, S. A. Rubby, A. K. Miller, J. K. Fleury, K. A. Chandler, M. G. Plany, and M. R. Rand. 2001. *Indicators of school crime and safety: 2001*. Washington, D.C.: U.S. Departments of Education and Justice. NCES 2002-113/NCJ-190075.

Rudo, Z. H., V. Robbins, and D. Smith. 2002. Addressing home, school, and community violence for children with disabilities. In J. L. Paul, C. D. Lavely, A. Cranston-Gingras, and E. L. Taylor, ed. *Rethinking professional issues in special education*. Westport, Connecticut: Ablex Publishing.

Snyder, H. 2002. *Juvenile Arrests 2000*. Washington, D.C.: Office of Juvenile Justice and Delinquency Prevention, at ojjdp.ncjrs.org/ojstatbb/html (accessed February 22, 2002).

U.S. Surgeon General. 2001. *Youth violence: A report of the surgeon general*. Washington, D.C.: U.S. Surgeon General Office, at surgeongeneral.gov. library/youthviolence/toc.html (accessed February 22, 2002).

Chapter One

Overview of Youth and School Violence

John King and James Hurst

Youth and school violence have affected the lives of U.S. school children in the last decade (Jenson and Howard 1999). The tragic school shootings in communities such as Littleton, Colorado; West Paducah, Kentucky; Jonesboro, Arkansas; and Carrolton, Georgia, have brought this to the forefront. These and other similar incidents have raised safety concerns and fears for everyone involved with schools (Reddy et al. 2001). Youth violence is a "high-priority" concern in every sector of the United States (U.S. Surgeon General 2001). The 2000 Annual Report of School Safety states that although youth violence and crime have declined in the United States, they remain one of the greatest challenges that our country faces (U.S. Department of Education 2000).

According to the U.S. Surgeon General (2001), even though the evidence suggests that youth violence is less lethal than it was in 1993, the percentage of adolescents involved in violent behavior remains alarmingly high. Regardless of the location and sources of youth violence, the consequences of this violence are proving to be devastating for children throughout our country (Jenson and Howard 1999). The first step toward preventing youth and school violence is to understand the origins of youth violence, its prevalence, and its causes and risk factors so that more effective, research-based strategies can be developed to address this problem (U.S. Surgeon General 2001).

MEASUREMENT OF YOUTH/SCHOOL VIOLENCE

Any discussion of youth and school violence must include an analysis of
the different studies, surveys, and other reports where data are gathered.
In the area of youth and school violence, there are two primary sources for
data: governmental data (arrest records, and so on) and self-report data
(surveys, and so on). Any source of data has inherent strengths and weak-
nesses. No single study or report can provide a completely accurate picture of any topic of research or study (U.S. Surgeon General 2001).

Advantages and Disadvantages of Using
Governmental Data Statistics

Governmental data sources are derived from official crime statistics com-
piled by law enforcement agencies and are usually based on arrest reports
(U.S. Surgeon General 2001). The main governmental data used in this
chapter were the reports of juvenile arrests published by the U.S. Department of Justice (Snyder 2000, 2002). These reports are based on the data
collected by the Federal Bureau of Investigation Uniform Crime Reporting Program (Snyder 2000). The purpose of this information is to charac-
terize the extent and nature of juvenile crime that comes to the attention
of the justice system (Snyder 2000). These governmental arrest reports
have clear advantages and disadvantages.

First, an advantage of these arrest reports is that they are specific and accurate about the number of crimes reported to the police. Second, they give
an accurate picture of the volume and types of arrests and how the volume
changes over time. Third, arrest reports are "reasonably valid ways of measuring the particular aspects of violence they were designed to measure"
(U.S. Surgeon General 2001, 3). Finally, an arrest report is an accurate
record of the flow into the criminal and judicial systems (Snyder 2000).
These data allowed the surgeon general to conclude that the decline in
youth crime from 1993 to 2000 can be partly attributed to police crack-
downs on weapon possession, gun purchase laws (illegal gun purchases),
and longer sentences for violent crimes (U.S. Surgeon General 2001).

Governmental arrest data, however, also have many limitations and disadvantages. First, this information reports only total arrests and does not
provide the number of individuals (Snyder 2000; U.S. Surgeon General

2001). For example, one person could be arrested several times in a year for various offenses and arrest records do not account for the fact that one individual was arrested for these offenses. Instead, it only counts as the total arrests in a year. Second, arrest reports account for only those crimes reported to the police (Snyder 2000; U.S. Surgeon General 2001). For example only 48 percent of all violent victimizations were reported to the police during 2000 (U.S. Department of Justice 2001).

Finally, the reports are not helpful in examining the prevalence of school violence. For example, some incidents of school violence might not be reported to the police because either the incidents lacked severity or the incidents were not brought to the attention of the school administration. On the other hand, acts of school violence such as fighting might warrant police intervention, but are dealt with by employing other types of school punishments (suspensions, expulsions, detentions, and so on). Both examples demonstrate school violence among youth, but are not found on arrest records because law enforcement authorities were not asked to intervene.

Despite the limitations, it appears that governmental arrest reports are the best measure of the justice system's response to observed or reported crime. They are not as helpful, however, with measuring school violence, the number of actual juveniles committing crimes, and the frequency of arrests that any particular juvenile receives during a given year (Snyder 2000; U.S. Surgeon General 2001).

Self-Report Statistics

Self-report statistics are reported directly by people and not by governmental agencies. They are usually seen in the form of surveys. These survey reports could be obtained either from the same group of people over a long period of time (longitudinal survey) or from different groups of people at the same point in time (cross-sectional survey). The advantage of a longitudinal study is that the same subjects are used in the study, which makes the results more accurate and reliable. The main disadvantages of longitudinal studies are that they are time-consuming and expensive to conduct, and subjects leave the study, which affects the reliability of the results. If these disadvantages can be minimized, longitudinal studies are the most desired research design. The advantages of cross-section designs are that they are less expensive, take less time, and produce results in different groups at the same time. The disadvantage is the use of different subjects, making generalizability and reliability of the results an issue. Cross-sectional studies are appropriate as long as measures are in place to ensure good reliability.

Self-report data, as also seen in governmental data, have their strengths and limitations. First, an advantage is that they can employ both cross-sectional and longitudinal design approaches (U.S. Surgeon General 2001). This creates a great deal of flexibility in the types of information that one can gather with regard to youth and school violence. Second, their confidential nature can help researchers get an accurate, honest picture of youth and school violent activity (U.S. Surgeon General 2001). Third, self-reports get the information directly from the student themselves, which is the best way to measure violent behavior that never reaches the judicial system (U.S. Surgeon General 2001). Fourth, it is the only way to accurately observe student perceptions on school and youth violence and school safety. Arrest report data, by their nature, cannot record, study, and evaluate the perceptions of students and faculty about the school environment. Fifth, self-report data can help provide a more accurate picture of youth and school violent crime, since arrest data reports, in general, underestimate the prevalence of crime (Snyder 2000; U.S. Surgeon General 2001).

With all the benefits of self-report data, there are some limitations. First, youths may fail to report their violent behavior accurately, either deliberately or because of faulty memory (U.S. Surgeon General 2001). Second, youths may exaggerate their involvement, reporting lesser events in response to more serious forms of violence (U.S. Surgeon General 2001). Third, great care needs to be taken with regard to correct sampling techniques so the results are representative of the population being studied (U.S. Surgeon General 2001). Finally, the confidentiality of the students must be protected in these self-report studies. Any breaches in confidentiality would compromise the accuracy and honesty of the information provided by the students (Coggeshall and Kingery 2001; U.S. Surgeon General 2001).

With regard to self-report data, if caution is given to confidentiality and random sampling, self-report surveys can provide accurate, honest information that cannot be gleaned from governmental arrest records. Both self-report and arrest records data contribute to understanding of youth and school violence (U.S. Surgeon General 2001).

In this chapter we use four main self-report surveys: the Monitoring the Future Survey (MTF), the Youth Risk Behavior Survey (YRBS), the National Criminal Victimization Survey (NCVS), and the Metropolitan Life Survey of the American Teacher 1999 and 2000 (MLSAT).

Monitoring the Future Survey (MTF)

The MTF survey is conducted by the Survey Research Center at the University of Michigan and is funded by the National Institute on Drug Abuse (Kingery and Coggeshall 2001). It is a cross-sectional design that has surveyed a large sample of high school seniors annually since 1975 (Coggeshall and Kingery 2001). Since 1991, samples of students in grades 8, 10, and 12 have also been included. The students are sampled to represent the forty-eight contiguous states (Johnston 2000). The MTF uses a three-stage cluster sampling design: select (a) primary sampling units (PSUs) with defined geographic boundaries, (b) schools within the selected PSUs, and (c) students within the selected schools (Johnston 2000). The survey is usually administered in the regular classrooms unless special provisions are needed for larger groups. Professional representatives of the survey are the administrators of the surveys. Currently the test is given anonymously to the 8th and 10th graders, but the 12th graders are surveyed confidentially (Johnston 2000).

An advantage of the MTF is that it asks a wide array of questions concerning violence, drug and alcohol use, educational information, work and leisure activities and plans, sex roles and family, conservation and materialism, religion, politics, military, interpersonal relationships, race relations, concern for others, happiness and other personality issues, deviance and victimization, and health (Johnston 2000). The variety of questions on this survey makes this a very important survey of youth behavior in the United States.

The MTF does have a couple of disadvantages. First, the public-use data files do not include the sampling-design variables required to compute accurate estimates with regard to variance (Coggeshall and Kingery 2001). The other disadvantage is that the 8th and 10th graders take the test anonymously and the 12th graders are given the test confidentially. There is some concern about the comparability of data from these two groups. Some questions might find underreported behaviors in the 12th graders due to the confidential nature of their survey, as opposed to the more candid responses of the anonymous nature of the 8th and 10th graders survey (Coggeshall and Kingery 2001). Overall, the MTF survey estimates are representative of the responses of the students in both public and private school nationwide (Kingery and Coggeshall 2001).

Youth Risk Behavior Survey (YRBS)

The YRBS is a survey administered by the Centers for Disease Control and Prevention (CDC) to a nationally representative sample of adolescents in grades 9–12 in both public and private school in the fifty states and the District of Columbia (Coggeshall and Kingery 2001). It was first conducted in 1990 and revised and fielded again in 1991. Since that time it has been administered biennially (Coggeshall and Kingery 2001). The sample is chosen using a three-stage stratified cluster design that randomly selects classrooms of students to complete the survey.

An advantage of the YRBS is that it allows the students to remain anonymous because it does not make any attempt to ask for any identifying information, nor does it make any attempt to link them to their responses (Coggeshall and Kingery 2001). According to Coggeshall and Kingery, an analytical advantage to the YRBS is that the public-use data files include the strata and primary sampling unit variables required to compute variance estimates that account for the complex sampling design. A major drawback of the YRBS is that it asks only ten questions (out of eighty total questions) about school violence (Coggeshall and Kingery 2001). This study is a self-report with valuable information regarding both violent behaviors and perceptions about youth and school violence.

National Criminal Victimization Survey (NCVS)

The NCVS is an ongoing study of criminal victimization among people age 12 and older living in households or group quarters in the fifty states and the District of Columbia (Coggeshall and Kingery 2001). It is sponsored by the U.S. Department of Justice and conducted by the Bureau of the Census. Households are selected in the sample by multistage cluster procedures and their members are interviewed seven times every six months for a period of three years. Five of the seven interviews are conducted by phone and the other two are conducted in person. The survey is designed to capture criminal incidents both reported and not reported to police. For a better understanding of school crime, the School Crime Supplement was added to the NCVS in 1989 and 1995.

An advantage of the NCVS is the sampling procedure and its attempt to glean a more accurate picture of criminal victimization in the United States. A disadvantage to the NCVS is the problem with the confidentiality of phone interviews. In fact, the results of reported criminal occurrences of the NCVS survey is uniformly lower than other surveys such as the Monitoring the Future (MTF) survey (Coggeshall and Kingery 2001).

Metropolitan Life Study of the American Teacher, 1999 and 2000 (MLSAT)

These surveys were conducted by Louis Harris and Associates for the Metropolitan Life Insurance Company. This MLSAT study was originally conducted in 1993 and the 1999 MLSAT study was conducted to compare self-report data about trends and perceptions from 1993–1998. These surveys were conducted in classrooms of 1,044 students in grades 3–12 (Metropolitan Life 1999). The sampling procedure was based on a stratified two-stage sampling design. This was to compare with the sample designs in various studies conducted by the U.S. National Center for Education Statistics. The 2000 MLSAT study was conducted from a nationally represented sample of 3,961 public school students and 1,010 public school teachers in grades 7–12 only (Metropolitan Life 2000). The 2000 study also included a nationally representative sample of 2,017 parents of public school students. The parents interviewed represented public school students from grades K–12. As in the 1999 MLSAT study, the sampling procedures were conducted in the same manner for the 2000 study.

There are some advantages to these studies. First, they include students from all levels (elementary through high school) and also include teachers, parents, and law enforcement officials. They provide a variety of perspectives toward the school violence issue. Second, much information can be gleaned regarding the perceptions of all populations associated with the school.

These surveys have some disadvantages, however. First, the way in which the surveys were administered causes some concern. The 1999 study was mailed out to the schools and the school self-administered the questionnaire. The 2000 study was a mix of self-administered written questionnaires and self-administered online questionnaires. In all of these instances, there can be questions about the errors made in the inconsistency of all of the classrooms following through with the survey and further inconsistencies with the administering of the survey from school to school. Overall, these survey are additional tools to gain a more complete picture of school violence trends from 1993–1998 (1999 MLSAT) and to provide a more accurate picture of current thinking in school violence (2000 MLSAT).

In this chapter, youth violence refers to the overall statistics, facts, trends, and information pertaining to juvenile behavior that is violent in nature. In governmental statistical data, juvenile crime (crimes committed by youth younger than 18) is organized in three categories, or indices: (a) Violent Crime, (b) Property Crime, and (c) Nonindex Crime (Snyder 2000). Moreover, the terms of youth and school violence will be used frequently. The statistical data in many of the studies and reports in this chapter include much information that applies to both youth and school violence.

Youth Violence Arrest Rates versus Self-Report Data

When estimating youth violence, it is important to keep in mind that statistics based on arrest rates only account for a portion of the total number of youth crimes reported to the police. More than 80 percent of chronic violent offenders are never arrested for a serious violent crime (U.S. Surgeon General 2001), and more than half of all violent victimizations were not reported to police for the year 2000 (U.S. Department of Justice 2001). Another limitation of current data is that they reflect only total arrests rather than the number of individuals arrested for different crimes (Snyder 2000). For example, a single perpetrator could be arrested three times for various offenses but arrest rates would not account for the fact that the same person committed all three crimes. Last, arrest notes may not be helpful in the school context. Many incidents of school violence might not be reported to the police because of either lack of severity or not being brought to the attention of school administrators. Some acts of school violence, such as fighting, might warrant police intervention if they occurred outside of school. The same violent acts, within the school setting, might be dealt with by employing various types of educational dispositions such as suspensions, expulsions, and detentions. Arrest data do not capture this type of violence. Despite these limitations, arrest reports are still considered "reasonably valid ways of measuring the particular aspects of violence they were designed to measure" (U.S. Surgeon General 2001).

Self-report data on violence such as the Monitoring the Future Survey (MTF) also have several limitations (U.S. Surgeon General 2001). Survey respondents might not be accurate in their reports due to exaggeration, under-reporting of violence, or memory problems. Also, sampling techniques need to be used with any survey, whereas arrest rates are aggregate numbers. Last, a recent study by Coggeshall and Kingery (2001) illustrates how respondents' concerns about confidentiality might affect self-report of violence. However, unlike arrest data, self-report data assess the youth's behavior and perceptions in a confidential manner, thereby providing a measure of the large amount of violent behavior that never reaches the judicial system. As noted earlier, the four self-report surveys cited frequently in the literature and cited in this chapter on youth violence are the Monitoring the Future Survey (MTF), the Youth Risk Behavior Survey (YRBS), the National Criminal Victimization Survey (NCVS), and the Metropolitan Life Study of the American Teacher 1999 (MLSAT).

YOUTH VIOLENCE: ARREST RATES

Youth violence is not a new phenomenon in our country with roots found early in our century (Jenson and Howard 1999). The first notable statistics in the last quarter-century came in 1978 upon the release of the Safe School Study Report to Congress. This report stated that 282,000 students and 5,200 teachers were physically assaulted in high school every month (National Institute of Education 1978; Elliott, Hamburg, and Williams 1998). During the late 1980s and early 1990s, the juvenile violence rates increased dramatically in the United States (Snyder 2002; Jenson and Howard 1999). This corresponded with the overall violence statistics in the United States during this same time period (Federal Bureau of Investigation 2000). As figure 1.1 shows, juvenile violent crime arrest rates between the years of 1987 and 1994 increased 68 percent (Snyder 2002). That pattern can also

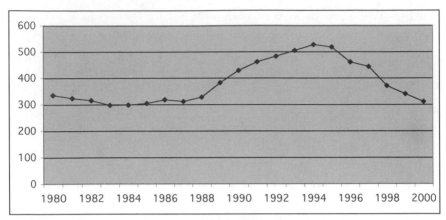

Figure 1.1. Violent Crime Index (Synder 2002. Reprinted with permission.)

be seen in the statistics pertaining to murder (see figure 1.2) and forcible rape (see figure 1.3), and aggravated assault (see figure 1.4) through the years of 1987–1994 (Snyder 2002).

As the governmental arrests data suggest, there has been a consistent pattern of youth violence in the main categories during the past twenty-five years. Regarding juvenile arrests from violent crimes, we see the following pattern: First, the rates showed a reasonable amount of consistency in the years 1973–1987, where it averaged 300 to 340 arrests per 100,000 juveniles ages 10–17 years (Snyder 2000). Second, we see a sharp increase in arrests in the years 1987–1994, with the rate peaking in 1994 and

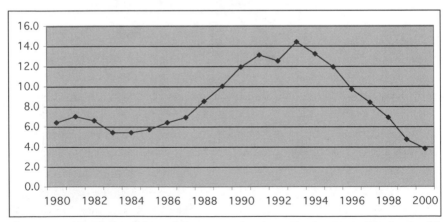

Figure 1.2. Murder and Nonnegligent Manslaughter (Synder 2002. Reprinted with permission.)

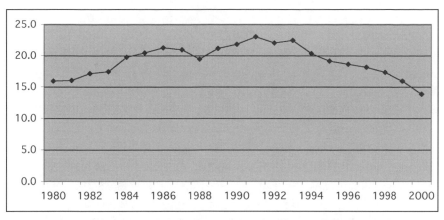

Figure 1.3.   Forcible Rape (Synder 2002. Reprinted with permission.)

exceeding 500 arrests for violent crimes per 100,000 juveniles ages 10–17 (Snyder 2000). Finally, the latest trend appears to be declining from 1996 to 2000 with a total decrease of 23 percent during these years (Snyder 2002). We can even see an additional decrease of 5 percent in juvenile violent crime from 1999 to 2000 (Snyder 2002).

Specifically, these trends can be seen in the governmental data in each category of juvenile violent crime. We can see similarities and differences in the trend of juvenile arrest rates for murder during this same time period. The first primary similarity between these statistics and the rates of the overall juvenile crime rate was the apparent increase in juvenile arrests

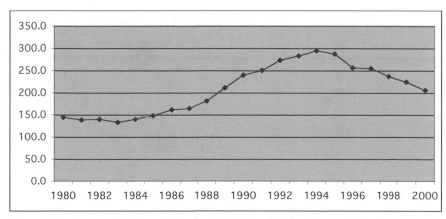

Figure 1.4.   Aggravated Assault (Synder 2002. Reprinted with permission.)

1984 to 1994. The rate of juvenile murder arrests during this period rose dramatically from 6 of every 100,000 youths to more than 14 of every 100,000 youths (Snyder 2000; Jenson and Howard 1999). With regard to juvenile arrests for murder, we can see a steady decline from 1993 to 1999 with a decrease of 23 percent from 1995 to 1999 and a decrease of 13 percent from 1999 to 2000 (Jenson and Howard 1999; Snyder 2000, 2002).

The same trend is evident regarding juvenile arrests for forcible rape. As figure 1.3 shows, a similar increase in juvenile arrests occurred during the time period of 1984–1993 for forcible rape, although these have not fluctuated as much as some of the other juvenile arrests statistics (Snyder 2002). These arrests show an increase from about 20 arrests per 100,000 juveniles in 1988 to about 23 arrests per 100,000 juveniles in 1991 and 1993 (Jenson and Howard 1999; Snyder 2000). These arrests also show a consistent downward trend from 1993 to 1997 from about 23 arrests per 100,000 in 1993 to 18 per 100,000 in 1997 (Snyder 2000). From 1996 to 2000 we have seen a further decrease of 17 percent in forcible rape arrests with a decrease of 5 percent from 1999 to 2000 (Snyder 2002).

Finally we can see this similar trend in arrest rates of juvenile arrests for aggravated assault (see figure 1.4) and robbery (see figure 1.5). First, we can see this similar pattern of consistency in the number of arrests from 1980 to around 1987 with the exception of the slight decrease in the robbery arrests in this time period. Overall, there is a sense of consistency in these rates and a level of similarity to the other juvenile crime categories during this period.

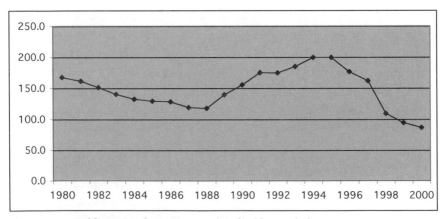

Figure 1.5.   Robbery (Synder 2002. Reprinted with permission.)

Second, this similarity in the trend can be seen in the increase of juvenile arrests of aggravated assault and robbery. With regard to aggravated assault, we see a dramatic increase of about 150 arrests per 100,000 juveniles in 1987 to 300 arrests per 100,000 juveniles (ages 10–17) in 1994 (Snyder 2000). We also see a pattern of increased juvenile arrests on robbery. There was an increase in juvenile robbery arrests from about 125 arrests per 100,000 in 1987 to 200 arrests per 100,000 in 1994 and 1995 (Snyder 2000). Finally, as in the other arrest categories, we see a decline in the number of arrests from the years 1994 to 2000. The arrests for aggravated assault decreased from about 300 arrests per 100,000 to 250 per 100,000 juveniles from 1994 to 1997 (Snyder 2000). We see this trend continue from 1996 to 2000 with the arrests rates decreasing a total of 14 percent, and a decrease of 4 percent from 1999 to 2000 (Snyder 2002). The juvenile arrest rates for robbery from 1996 to 2000 have shown an even more dramatic overall decline. The arrests for juvenile robbery have decreased 38 percent during this time period and have even decreased 5 percent from 1999 to 2000 (Snyder 2002). Juvenile robbery arrest rates, however, have shown the greatest level of consistency from 1970 to 2000, as compared with the other juvenile violent crime categories.

It is important to discuss that the statistics concerning youth weapon possession arrests in this section. In 1980 the arrest rates for weapons law violations for juveniles ages 10–17 years was 91.9 per 100,000 persons. These rates stayed steady until 1985 (109.8 per 100,000) to 1993 (224.4 per 100,000) (Snyder 2002). This represented an increase of approximately 200 percent in juvenile weapon arrests. This rise is attributed to the burgeoning crack cocaine epidemic, the rise of gang violence in urban areas, and the increase of production of inexpensive handguns in the United States (U.S. Surgeon General 2001). This trend from 1980 to 1993 parallels most of the other governmental data pertaining to youth violence during this time period. From 1993 to 2000, we see a trend of decreased juvenile weapons law arrests. The data show a decline of 224.4 arrests per 100,000 persons in 1993 to 116.6 per 100,000 in 2000 (Snyder 2002). This represents a decrease of 192 percent from 1993 to 2000 in juvenile weapons law arrests. This drop is attributed to changes in laws in weapon prosecution and various gun laws in the United States (U.S. Surgeon General 2001). This arrest data

demonstrated a decrease that paralleled the trends in overall youth violence and in each separate category of youth violence in the United
States during 1993 to 2000.

YOUTH VIOLENCE: COMPARISON OF SELF-REPORT
VERSUS ARREST DATA

It can be clearly seen, according to the governmental arrest data, that
youth violent crime has generally been on the decline since 1994; however, the self-report data does not show the same results. The Monitoring
the Future Survey (MTF), a self-report survey conducted by the University of Michigan, shows some different data about youth violence. First,
their results on overall violence show a peak around 1990 with just less
than 40 percent reported rate of prevalence of 12th graders (Johnston
2000). Second, the decline as seen in the governmental data in the later
1990s is seen to only a small degree. There is a decline in the prevalence
rate of violence among high school seniors from 1991 to 1995, but these
self-reports show another increase from about 30 percent to 33 percent
from 1995 to 1998 (Johnston 2000).

Third, we see a steady pattern of youth robbery with a weapon from
the MTF study from 1980 to 1998. If there is any trend from this category it would be a very slight increase, but for the most part, this area
has remained steady during the past twenty years. Fourth, we see a
moderate increase in assault with injury in this study during the past
twenty years (Johnston 2000). This does not coincide with the trend of
an increase in the late 1980s and early 1990s following a decrease
through the later 1990s, as demonstrated from the governmental data
discussed earlier. The self-report data of high school seniors do not
echo the results as seen in the governmental arrest data. Finally, we see
inconsistency with the self-report data concerning weapons possession
and the governmental arrest data of weapons law arrests. Even though
the arrest data show a decrease in lethal violent acts with weapons and
a decline in weapons law arrests, self-report surveys of high school seniors show no change in the percentage that have been injured with a
weapon at school (about 5 percent) from 1976 to 1998 (U.S. Surgeon
General 2001).

SCHOOL VIOLENCE

In general, schools are usually much safer for youth than nonschool settings and have significantly fewer acts of serious violence compared with homes and neighborhoods (U.S. Surgeon General 2001). In recent years, however, the well-publicized school shooting events, such as the Columbine High School tragedy, have dominated the school violence focus in the media and in the public (Astor et al. 1999). Overall, as in general youth violence, many of the statistics do not support this public and media perception of an increase in school violence in recent years (Kaufman et al. 2001; Reddy et al. 2000; U.S. Department of Education 2000). For example, between 1995 and 1999 the percentage of students who reported being victims of crime at school decreased from 10 percent to 8 percent (Kaufman et al. 2001). Specifically, between 1995 and 1999, the prevalence of reported youth victimization dropped from 11 percent to 8 percent for 7th-grade students, 11 percent to 8 percent for 8th-grade students, and 12 percent to 9 percent for high school freshmen (Kaufman et al. 2001).

Although violent deaths at school have caused the most concern in the public and media, they are a very small percentage of the overall violent death rate for youths. Approximately 1 percent of all murders occurred in a school setting from 1998 to 1999 (Kaufman et al. 2001; National School Safety Center 2000). In fact, the total number of violent death incidents has declined from a high of 49 in the 1995–1996 school year to 34 during the 1998–1999 school year (U.S. Department of Education 2000).

There are also statistics, however, that do cause concern for the need for increased efforts to improve student safety at school. For example, between 1993 and 1999, the percentage of high school students (grades 9–12) who were threatened or injured with a weapon on school property in the prior twelve months remained at a constant 7 percent to 8 percent (Kaufman et al. 2001). In 1999 (the most recent year that data were available for this review), approximately 7 percent of students reported recently carrying a weapon on school property and more than 17 percent reputed reported recently carrying a weapon at or away from school (Division of Adolescent and School Health 1999). Also in 1998, more than 14 percent of students reported being in one or more physical fights at school in the prior 12-month period (Division of Adolescent and School

Health 1999). Including violent crimes and theft, students 12–18 years of age were victims of 2.5 million crimes at school during the year. From 1993 to 1999, teachers were victims of 1.7 million violent crimes or thefts (Kaufman et al. 2001). Last, from 1993 to 1999, alcohol and marijuana use (major risk factors for violence for younger children) either increased or stayed the same for 9th through 12th grades (Kaufman et al. 2001).

General School Violence

Discussion of school violence must begin with the broad topic of school violence. As mentioned earlier, school violence can include the following issues: murder, carrying weapons, bullying, verbal threats/intimidation, gang violence, rape, hate crimes, vandalism, and dating violence (Astor et al. 1999). In this area of discussion, we will focus on the violent crimes (murder, forcible rape/sexual assault, robbery, and aggravated assault). We will also examine fighting because of its escalatory nature to more se-vere forms of violence.

Overall, the governmental statistical data suggest that trends of school violence parallel juvenile crime away from school and violent crime lev-els for adults (Kaufman et al. 2001). We can see a similarity with youth nonfatal crime that the totals peak in 1993–1994 and steadily decline from 1994 to 1998 (U.S. Surgeon General 2001). The same can also be seen on theft, violent crime, and serious violent crime. We see the earlier trend of a peaking in these areas in 1993–1994 followed by a steady decrease in crime from 1993–1999 both at school and away from school (Kaufman et al. 2001).

Youth murders have declined 27 percent from 1996 to 2000 (Snyder 2002). This can be seen in schools as well. The school-associated death rate peaked in the years 1992 to 1994 (65 and 53 deaths) and has shown a decrease from 1994 to 1999 (average of 26.6 school-associated violent deaths from 1994–1999) (National School Safety Center 2000). It is im-portant to note that these overall numbers for school killings is so small that conceptualizing them in terms of rates or averages can be misleading. In the 1998–1999 school year there were 2,407 youth murders and only 33 (1.3 percent) of these murders occurred at school (Kaufman et al. 2001). In the 1998–1999 school year there were 1,854 youth suicides, and only 4 (.21 percent) occurred at school. Anderson et al. (2001) reviewed all school-associated violent deaths (including suicides) from 1994–1999 and found that the rate of single-victim student homicides decreased significantly during this time period, while multiple-victim events increased. The total amount of deaths documented in this study (n = 253) was still below 1 percent of the violent deaths for all students. As these numbers indicate, school-associated murders are rare, have decreased during the last several years, and make up a very small percentage of overall deaths among youths (Kaufman et al. 2001; National School Safety Center 2000; Snyder 2002).

With regard to theft, we see this similar trend both in school and away from school. There is a peak in thefts in 1992 and a steady decrease from 1992 to 1999 (Kaufman et al. 2001). It is important to note, however, that students were more likely to be a victim of theft at school than away from school, which is a concern to schools and school safety (Kaufman et al. 2001). It is encouraging to see the decrease from just less than 100 crimes per 1,000 students in 1992 to near 60 crimes per 1,000 students in 1999 (Kaufman et al. 2001).

We see this trend with regard to the nonfatal serious violent crimes among students both in and away from school (Kaufman et al. 2001). Included in the category of serious violent crimes as rape, sexual assault, and aggravated assault (robbery is included in this category, but we included it with the discussion of theft). First, these crimes peaked around 1994 (13 per 1,000 students) and have steadily decreased from 1993 to 1999 (7 per 1,000 students). Second, the rate of serious violent crime associated with school has always been lower than serious violent crime away from school (Kaufman et al. 2001). Finally, all the indicators of school violent crime have decreased from 1993–1999, although some of the categories have shown a very gradual decrease (Kaufman et al. 2001).

The arrest and self-report data show no change in the prevalence of students being threatened or injured with a weapon on school property in the last twelve months from 1993 to 1999—about 7 percent to 8 percent (Division of Adolescent and School Health 1999; Kaufman et al. 2001). This does not parallel with the decrease in juvenile weapons law arrests from 1994 to 1999, as discussed earlier in this chapter. Second, the arrest data and self-report data both show a decrease in students carrying a weapon on school property (12 percent to 7 percent) and carrying a weapon anywhere (22 percent to 17 percent) from 1993 to 1999 (Division of Adolescent and

School Health 1999; Kaufman et al. 2001). This does parallel the arrest data that show a decrease of weapon possession arrests from 1993 to 2000 (Snyder 2002). In the Metropolitan Life Insurance Company report (1999) Harris and Associates report that 12 percent of all public school students have carried a weapon to school at some point and 59 percent of all public school students report that at least some students in their school regularly carry weapons.

Overall, the evidence of students carrying weapons at school before 1993 is unclear because some of the self-report studies such as the Monitoring the Future and Youth Risk Behavior Survey did not consistently ask these questions until the mid-1990s (U.S. Surgeon General 2001). The evidence from 1993 to 2000, however, is showing an encouraging trend, although more emphasis needs to be placed in this area of youth and school violence.

TARGETED SCHOOL VIOLENCE

The well-publicized school shootings during the last decade have more recently been studied by researchers looking for trends and patterns among the perpetrators of these acts. Previous work by Elliott et al. (1998) conceptualized youth violence among four patterns: (a) situational (where the specific situations or context is dominant); (b) relationships (occurring within the specific context of an existing relationship); (c) predatory (antisocial violence associated with some type of gain); and (d) psychopathological (rare acts related directly to mental disorders.) However, this does not provide an adequate heuristic for beginning to understand how the school shootings are qualitatively different from most all other serious youth violence including murders. With research in the early stages in this area, it does appear that these types of school shootings differed in substantial ways from the more common and less publicized types of youth violence previously discussed.

The U.S. Secret Service is studying these school shootings and has used the term *targeted violence* to differentiate some of the school shootings from others (Reddy et al. 2001; Vossekuil et al. 2000).

According to the Secret Service, the term *targeted school violence* refers to "any incident of violence where a known (or knowable) attacker selects a particular target prior to their violent attack" (Vossekuil et al. 2000, 1). This target may be an identified (or identifiable) person, such as a particular schoolmate or teacher, or it could be a building, such as the school itself (Vossekuil et al. 2000). School shootings (assassinations), such as the Columbine tragedy in 1999, are examples of targeted school violence. Other targeted violence includes some types of school violence, workplace violence, and many types of stalking (Vossekuil et al. 2000).

Fortunately, all types of targeted violence, either in the workplace or in the schools, are rare (Vossekuil et al. 2000). Regarding targeted school violence, we have seen statistics in the general school violence section to support the rarity of this type of violence (1.3 percent of all youth murders were targeted in 1999) (Kaufman et al. 2001; National School Safety Center 2000). Even though targeted school violence is a much less serious threat to today's youth compared with other school violence, the tremendous effect that these events have on the school, community, and the nation is enormous, prompting many communities to implement plans to prevent these types of incidents in their communities (Reddy et al. 2001; Vossekuil et al. 2000).

Targeted school violence, contrary to common belief, is not a new phenomenon (Vossekuil et al. 2000). The first case that was examined occurred in 1974, when a student brought guns and homemade bombs to his school, pulled the fire alarm, and shot adults (janitors and firemen) who responded to the alarm (Vossekuil et al. 2000). Since this first case there have been thirty-seven identified incidents involving forty-one attackers and have taken place in a total of twenty-six states (Vossekuil et al. 2000). As with school deaths in general, these numbers are so small as to make identifying trends and patterns a tentative process. This caution is also reflected in the individualized approach of threat assessment recommended by the authors to prevent targeted violence (Reddy et al. 2001). In more than two-thirds of these incidents, the attacker killed one or more students, faculty, or others at the school and guns were the primary weapon used (Vossekuil et al. 2000).

Last, the authors acknowledge that the concept and definition of target violence is in development and is currently somewhat vague. For example, shootings that are clearly related to gang or drug activity would not be classified as targeted violence (Vossekuil et al. 2000), but the definition would not necessarily exclude such contexts. It appears that targeted attackers do not share many of the correlates and risk factors for general violence described in the next section of this chapter. Vossekuil et al. (2000), notes the following proposed differences between targeted and nontargeted attackers:

- There was no typical age. Attackers ranged from 11 to 21 years old.
- Attackers came from a variety of racial and ethnic backgrounds.
- Attackers came from a variety of family backgrounds.
- Their academic performances ranged from excellent to failing.
- Their peer ties ranged from socially isolated to popular.
- Their behavioral histories varied from no apparent problems to repeated problems with disciplinary action.
- Fewer than a third of the attackers had a history of substance abuse.

PERCEPTIONS OF SCHOOL VIOLENCE

In general, students' and teachers' perceptions of school violence are mixed. On the positive side there have been some improvements from 1995 to 1999 regarding students' perceptions of safety at school and when traveling to and from school (U.S. Department of Justice 2001). Students ages 12 to 18 who avoided one or more places in school decreased from 9 percent in 1995 to 5 percent in 1999. In 1998, nearly every public school teacher (99 percent) and most public school students (92 percent) felt safe at school, and both groups believed that school violence had decreased since 1995 (Metropolitan Life 1999). The 2000 MLSAT survey still shows that nearly nine of every ten (89 percent) of all surveyed public school students feel safe at school.

With all of these encouraging signs about the perceptions of school safety, there are many signs that the picture is not so promising. A variety of self-report surveys suggests either no change or a worsening of public perceptions of school violence. First, although the numbers have fluctuated from year to year, there has been a slight increase in the percentage of students who did not go to school one or more of the past thirty days because they felt unsafe, from 4.4 percent in 1993 to 5.2 percent in 1999 (Division of Adolescent and School Health 1999). Second, the percentage of students who have been threatened or injured with weapons on school property one or more times in the past twelve months has not decreased since 1997 (Metropolitan Life 1999). Third, the percentage of public school teachers that are worried about being physically attacked in or around school increased from 67 percent in 1993 to 76 percent in 1998 (Metropolitan Life 1999). Fourth, the percentage of public school students who rated themselves either "not very worried" or "not at all worried" about being physically attacked in or around school decreased from 77 percent in 1993 to 67 percent in 1999 (Metropolitan Life 1999).

The current MLSAT study (2000) creates even more concern about current perceptions about school safety and the role of the schools to help in this matter. Forty-four percent of public school parents believe that keeping schools safe (16 percent) and having people get along with each other (28 percent) are important issues facing the educational system today (Metropolitan Life 2000). Along this topic, 41 percent of public school students feel that keeping schools safe (18 percent) and having people get along with each other (23 percent) were important for the quality of education to improve in their schools (Metropolitan Life 2000). Approximately one-third of public school teachers (33 percent) believed that keeping schools safe and having people get along with each other were important issues to increase the quality of education in our schools (Metropolitan Life 2000). Overall, with regard to school safety and teaching people to better get along, 37 percent of all public school secondary school students, 38 percent of all secondary school parents, and 29 percent of all public school secondary teachers give their schools a report card grade of a C or lower (Metropolitan Life 2000).

Other statistics show a need for continued concern. Even though the number of public school students that feel safe was high in 1999 (92 percent), this perception has dropped 3 percent in one year to 89 percent in 2000 (1999). Second, the percentage of teachers that feel safe at school decreased form 99 percent in 1999 to 83 percent in 2000 (Metropolitan Life 1999 and 2000).

A final area of concern toward the school environment is trust and predictions toward the future. First, concerning the issue of trust, four out of every ten (39 percent) students trust their teachers only a little or not at all and four times as likely "to express this low level of trust about their teachers as they are about their family and friends" (Metropolitan Life 2000, 62). Finally, only 46 percent of the students, 26 percent of parents, and 39 percent of interviewed teachers believe that schools will become safer in the students' lifetimes (Metropolitan Life 2000).

CONCLUSION

Even though the data that exist regarding school violence and school safety are extensive, some conclusions can be gleaned from the information discussed in this chapter. First, the statistics on school violence show that our schools are safe. Regarding targeted school violence (school shootings, etc.), students are very safe. Statistics show that these tragic occurrences are, fortunately, very rare events.

Second, the statistics show school violence, as well as overall violence in the United States, increased dramatically from the middle of the 1980s to the early 1990s. From the middle 1990s to present, there has been a steady decline in school violence as well as overall violence in the United States. Even though all of the individual statistics show some slight variations, this is the general trend that can be gleaned from the governmental data discussed earlier in the chapter.

Third, although the statistics show a decline in school violence and safety, there are still many signs for continued concern in our educational system. As seen earlier, there are many statistical categories where school violence has either stayed the same or has increased. This is also reinforced by various self-report studies that show a higher level of public concern about school safety from student, parents, and teachers alike. This concern demonstrates an underlying concern about student safety, despite many of the discussed statistics.

Fourth, it is important to point to the 2000 MLSAT study of the public future confidence of future school safety. This pessimistic view of any future changes in school safety is a concern to everyone interested in the issue of school violence and safety. More research is needed to investigate.

Finally, the issue of trust deserves to be mentioned, as stated in the 2000 MLSAT study. There is a genuine concern that our educational system is not doing enough to create a safer, more secure environment. There is concern when 39 percent of the interviewed students do not feel they can trust their teachers (Metropolitan Life 2000). This concern can also be seen in the statistic that approximately one of three students, parents, and teachers do not feel that schools are doing enough to help students learn to get along with each other (Metropolitan Life 2000). This data truly suggest that our educational systems are not fully succeeding in creating a physically and emotionally safe learning environment for today's youth.

Perhaps schools need to examine what they do to include all students and to help these young people feel welcomed, needed, and to share a sense of belonging. These ideals parallel President George Bush's educational theme of "Leave no child behind."

Overall, even though there are statistics that suggest a safe school environment, there is a significant undercurrent of concern about our schools. Our schools need to do more to decrease the occurrences and severity of school violence and to promote an emotionally, as well as physically, safe school environment for today's youth.

REFERENCES

Anderson, M., J. Kaufman, T. R. Simon, L. Barrios, L. Paulozzi, G. Ryan, R. Hammond, W. Modzeleski, T. Feucht, L. Potter, and the School-Associated Violent Deaths Study Group. 2001. School-associated violent deaths in the United States 1994–1999. *Journal of the American Medical Association* 286(21): 2695–702.

Astor, R. A., L. A. Vargas, R. O. Pitner, and H. A. Meyer. 1999. School violence: Research, theory, and practice. In *Youth violence: Current research and recent practice innovations,* ed. J. M. Jenson and M. O. Howard, pp. 139–71. Washington, D.C.: NASW Press.

Coggeshall, M. B., and P. M. Kingery. 2001. Cross-sectional survey analysis of school violence and disorder. *Psychology in the Schools* 38(2): 107–16.

Derzon, J. H. 2001. Antisocial behavior and the prediction of violence: A meta-analysis. *Psychology in the Schools* 38: 93–106.

Division of Adolescent and School Health. 1999. *1999 National school-based youth risk behavior survey.* Washington, D.C.: Centers for Disease Control and Prevention, www.cdc.gov/nccdphp/dash/yrbs/survey99.htm (accessed March 9, 2002).

Elliott, D. S., B. A. Hamburg, and K. R. Williams. 1998. Violence in American schools: An overview. In *Violence in American schools,* ed. D. S. Elliott, B. A. Hamburg, and K. R. Williams, pp. 3–28. New York: Cambridge University Press.

Federal Bureau of Investigation. 2000. *Crime in the United States 2000: Uniform crime reports.* Washington, D.C.: U.S. Government Printing Office.

Howard, M. O., and J. M. Jenson. 1999. Cause of youth violence. In *Youth violence: Current research and recent practice innovations,* ed. J. M. Jenson and M. O. Howard, pp. 19–42. Washington, D.C.: NASW Press.

Jenson, J. M., and M. O. Howard. 1999. Prevalence and patterns of youth violence. In *Youth Violence: Current Research and Recent Practice Innovations,* ed. J. M. Jenson and M. O. Howard, pp. 3–18. Washington, D.C.: NASW Press.

Johnston, L. D. 2000. *Monitoring the future survey: National results on adolescent drug use.* Washington, D.C.: U.S. Department of Health and Human Services, National Institute of Health, http://monitoringthefuture.org (accessed March 27, 2002).

Kaufman, P., X. Chen, S. P. Choy, K. Peter, S. A. Ruddy, A. K. Miller, J. K. Fleury, K. A. Chandler, M. G. Plany, and M. R. Rand. 2001. *Indicators of school crime and safety: 2001.* Washington D.C.: U.S. Departments of Education and Justice. NCES 2002-113/NCJ-190075.

Kingery, P. M., and M. B. Coggeshall. 2001. Surveillance of school violence, injury, and disciplinary actions. *Psychology in the Schools* XXXVIII(2): 117–26.

Metropolitan Life Insurance Company. 1999. *The Metropolitan Life survey of the American teacher, 1999: Violence in America's public schools, five years later.* New York: Louis Harris and Associates.

Metropolitan Life Insurance Company. 2000. *The Metropolitan Life survey of the American teacher, 2000: Are we preparing students for the 21st century?* New York: Louis Harris and Associates.

National Institute of Education. 1978. *Violent school-safe schools: The safe school study report to Congress.* Washington D.C.: U.S. Department of Education.

National School Safety Center. 2000. *School associated violent deaths.* (Electronic Data Set), www.nssc1.org (accessed December 21, 2001).

Reddy, M., R. Borum, J. Berglund, B. Vossekuil, R. Fein, and W. Modzeleski. 2001. Evaluating risk for targeted violence in schools: Comparing risk assessment, threat assessment, and other approaches. *Psychology in the Schools* XXXVIII(2): 157–72.

Snyder, H. 2000. *Juvenile Arrests 1999.* Washington, D.C.: Office of Juvenile Justice and Delinquency Prevention.

Snyder, H. 2002. *Juvenile Arrests 2000.* Washington, D.C.: Office of Juvenile Justice and Delinquency Prevention, http://ojjdp.ncjrs.org/ojstatbb/html (accessed April 4, 2002).

U.S. Department of Justice. 2001. *National crime victimization survey: Criminal victimization 2000, changes 1999–2000 with trends 1993–2000.* Bureau of Justice Statistics and Office of Justice Programs. Washington, D.C. (June 2001). NCJ18007.

U.S. Department of Education. 2000. *2000 annual report on school safety.* Washington, D.C.: U.S. Department of Education, Education Publications Center.

U.S. Surgeon General. 2001. *Youth violence: A report of the surgeon general.* Washington D.C.: U.S. Surgeon General Office, http://surgeongeneral.gov. library/youthviolence/toc.html (accessed April 3, 2002).

Vossekuil, B., M. Reddy, R. Fein, R. Borum, and W. Modzeleski. 2000. *United States secret service safe school initiative: An interim report on the prevention of targeted violence in schools.* Washington D.C.: U.S. Secret Service, National Threat Assessment Center.

Chapter Two

Risk Factors Contributing to Youth and School Violence

James Hurst, John King, and Denise Smith

No single sign or set of early warning signs can accurately predict whether a child will be violent (Dwyer and Osher 2000; U.S. Surgeon General 2001). Research suggests, however, that certain risk factors may result in youth/school violence. Therefore, even though it is not possible to predict when a child will become violent, it is important to know the risk factors contributing to school and youth violence. The U.S. Surgeon General (2001) defined *risk factors* as "anything that increases the possibility that a person will suffer from harm" (57). The purpose of this chapter is to describe risk factors contributing to youth and school violence. The risk factors are reported in five domains: individual, family, peer group, community, and school.

INDIVIDUAL

General Offenses

Mitchell and Rosa (1979) found a relationship between early antisocial behavior (i.e., stealing and destruction of property) and violent behavior. For children 6–11 years old, committing general offenses is one of the strongest predictors for engaging in future behavior (Lipsey and Derzon 1998). Such offenses include violent acts as well as serious nonviolent crimes involving people or property. Regarding violent behavior, in general, prior violence has been established as one of the strongest predictors of later violence in children and adults (Borum 2000.) Early onset of serious nonviolent delinquent behaviors often progresses in severity to violent behavior. Loeber and Stouthamer-Loeber (1998) note that it is rare for youth to begin their delinquency with serious violent acts. Instead, they describe a model in which youth gradually increase the severity of their offenses along developmental pathways, which may end in violence, depending on the age and onset of the problem behaviors. For early adolescents (age 12–14), involvement in general offenses decreases as a predictor for violence, partly due to the fact that more youth from this age group are likely to engage in both violent and nonviolent offenses as compared with 6–11-year-olds (U.S. Surgeon General 2001). Derzon (2001) identified three variables—severity of crime, recidivism, (i.e., being in multiple fights, hitting a teacher on three or more occasions), and prior criminal activity—to be significant predictors for later violence. The majority of the subjects of this meta-analysis who displayed these behaviors went on to commit a violent or threatening act. However, a main point of this study was that many other antisocial and substance abusing behaviors (i.e., fighting, tobacco use) are not as accurate predictors because most young people who commit these acts do not engage in later violence. In other words, even though antisocial and substance-abusing behaviors are, in general, among the strongest predictors for later violence, one should not assume an overly simplistic direct relationship to violence for even many of these specific predictors.

Substance Use

Meta-analytic studies identify substance use (illicit drug use, alcohol use, or tobacco use) in younger children to be another one of the strongest predictors of later violence. One explanation for this relatively strong association is that substance abuse and violence share many of the same risk factors for youth. In their review, Moran and Jenson (1999) identified 25 risk factors across the five domain areas, which apply to both substance abuse and violence. Examples of these shared risk factors are hyperactivity (individual domain), and low school commitment (school domain). The authors also cite more than fifteen studies, which support the idea of shared risk factors for substance abuse and violence. For 6–11-year-olds, it seems reasonable to suspect that substance use would be associated with other delinquent behaviors, all stemming from shared risk factors. For example, most 8-year-olds do not even occasionally experiment with alcohol or drugs. Yet a hyperactive 8-year-old who comes from an antisocial, substance-abusing family, and associates with older substance-abusing and delinquent peers, is at risk for developing both substance use and violent behavior.

Substance use/abuse for 12–14-year-olds is a notably weaker predictor for later violence than if it were to have occurred at a younger age. Many more adolescents experiment and use alcohol, drugs, or tobacco than younger children. Moreover, most adolescents who engage in violence also engage in substance use; in fact, the U.S. Surgeon General's report (2001) identified these two areas as major co-occurring problem behaviors. Shared risk factors could be at work with adolescents just as easily as with younger children, but it may be more difficult to identify these cases due to the much larger number of adolescents engaging in some degree of substance use. Other research has examined the idea that direct or mediated effects of substances lead to aggressive and violent behavior. However, the results of this research are mixed and inconclusive partly due to the situational nature of their type of substance use–violence conceptualization.

Unlike many of the indicators for youth violence, substance use among young people does not appear to have declined during the last five to ten years. Instead, increases have occurred in drug-abuse arrests, and the availability of drugs within schools is cited earlier in this book. Alcohol and marijuana use are not declining. Given the evidence for shared common risk factors for substance use and violence, the lack of a decline in substance use is a significant concern for the area of youth violence.

Other types of drug-related behavior are associated with violence other than substance use. Hawkins et al. (1998) found that involvement in drug-selling at ages 14 and 16 tripled the risk for violent behavior by age 18. Within the community domain, the same study noted an increased risk for later violence for 14- and 16-year-olds who had drugs (marijuana and cocaine) available to them in their neighborhood.

Media Violence as a Risk Factor

Media violence includes depictions of varying degrees of violence in television, films, video games, music, and the Internet. In the wake of the

targeted school shootings of the 1990s, and especially the Columbine attack, media violence was widely touted as a cause in these tragedies (Anderson and Dill 2000; Mifflin 1999). The tendency of people to focus on
the media as a risk factor is understandable for three reasons. First, more
than most other risk factors, media violence cuts across the domains of the
individual, family, school, and community. For many Americans, media
violence may be one of the few risk factors that they observe in their daily
lives. For example, an older, childless, middle-class couple may have little first-hand knowledge or contact with drugs or gangs, but they can
easily notice increasing violence in their movies and television shows.
Second, in reaction to traumatic incidents such as target school shootings,
human beings tend to focus on broad, vaguely defined causes, rather than
more specific and complex factors, which might not be easily communi-
cated to the public. Third, and perhaps most important, many researchers
and professional organizations have indeed highlighted media violence as
a significant risk factor and have recommended changes in how the media portrays violence (APA 1993; Smith and Donnerstein 1998).

The empirical evidence for media violence as a risk factor for youth violence is mitigated by the fact that most of the research has used a range
of outcomes involving physical, verbal, or cognitive aggression rather
than the types of serious acts of violence highlighted in the U.S. Surgeon
General's report (2001). The link between television violence and youth
aggression is well established. However, the evidence for a relationship
between television violence and actual violent behavior is more tenuous.
In their meta-analysis of the effects of television violence, Paik and Comstock (1994) found moderate effect sizes for aggressive outcomes and
small effect sizes for serious forms of violence.

The effects of exposure to other forms of media violence (video games,
the Internet, and music videos) are less clear than television/film violence
mainly because of the scant number of research studies completed to date.
In a review of video games and aggression, Bensley and Van Eenuyk
(2001) found several experimental studies showing increased aggressive
behavior in young children immediately following video game play. However, with regard to teenagers, no conclusions could be drawn due to the
lack of experimental studies with that age group.

Similarly, the U.S. Surgeon General's report (2001) noted the lack of
published studies examining the relationship between violence in Web-

based media or music videos, and physical aggression. Last, a systematic review of the psychological literature on youth violence found only twenty-three studies (about .2 percent of total articles on youth violence), which focused on *any* type of media violence during 1980–1999 (Acosta et al. 2001). The same review noted that only four of the twenty-three studies examined prevention of media violence exposure. It appears that empirical studies of media violence in general and new media violence (video games, Internet, and music videos) in particular are sorely lacking in the recent literature.

Given that a main purpose for researching, conceptualizing, and prioritizing risk factors is to lay the foundation for effective intervention targets and programs, it is notable that none of the effective interventions in the U.S. Surgeon General's report (2001) focus on media violence. Conversely, risk factors such as substance abuse and bullying are not only effective targets for intervention programs, but, unlike watching a violence-laced television show, they are dangerous and unhealthy behaviors even apart from their effects on youth violence. Still, there is a strong research consensus that children's exposure to media violence can cause increased aggression both in the short term and the long term. As one prominent researcher in the area stated, "Media and cultural influences are not necessarily the most potent, but they are one of the most pervasive influences on children" (Mifflin 1999).

Gender

Males commit the vast majority of violent acts. This is true for both adults and adolescents. Likewise, most research studies in youth violence focus on studying and interpreting male violent behavior. Both official arrest rates and self-report data show that girls differ significantly from boys both in frequency and severity of violent acts (Potter 1999). However, female violent offending is increasing in the United States and Canada (Potter 1999; Leschied et al. 2001). Arrest rates for violent crimes committed by girls increased 25 percent from 1992 to 1996 (Budnick and Shields-Fletcher 1998). This trend is especially notable given the decrease in overall youth violence arrests during this same time period. With regard to risk factors, Potter (1999) noted in a recent review that while it is likely that girls and boys differ in how they offend, there is a lack of knowledge regarding predictors of violence in girls. As noted earlier, aggression has been identified as a pre-dictor of later violence for boys, but not for girls. Regarding correlates of youth violence, girls engage in less substance use and are less likely to show relationships between offending and school functioning (Huizinga and Jokob-Chien 1998). It is known that in disruptive behavior disorders, boys are more likely to externalize by engaging in acts such as fighting, stealing, and destructiveness, whereas girls are more likely to internalize in ways such as withdrawal, physical complaints, and experiencing anxiety (Kazdin 1995). Moreover, *relational aggression*, which involves the manipulation of peer relationships in ways such as exclusion from a social group or spread-ing negative gossip, appears to be much more prevalent in girls as compared with boys (Crick and Grotpeter 1995).

Aggression/Bullying

Aggression is defined in the Lipsey and Derzon (1998) study as including aggressive and disruptive behavior, aggression towards objects, and ver-bal aggression. It was found to have moderate predictive power for later violence among 6- to 11-year-olds and slightly less predictive power for the 12- to 14-year-old age group. As with substance use, the U.S. Surgeon General's report (2001) notes that this decrease in predictiveness for ado-lescents may be related to the fact that aggressiveness is much more com-mon in adolescents than in younger children.

Aggression and antisocial behavior are often conceptualized in similar ways, but Lipsey and Derzon (1998) distinguish between aggression and problem behavior, the latter of which includes aggressive inclinations and antisocial behavior. Hawkins et al. (1998) note several studies which show a consistent connection between aggression in young males and later violence. These authors go on to note that while early aggression is a predictor, it does not explain later violence since both variables are part of the same underlying construct.

Bullying is defined as specific types of aggressive behavior in which there is an imbalance of power and which occurs repeatedly over time. Three types of bullying are described by Ericson (2001): (a) physical bullying, which consists of hitting, kicking, spitting, pushing, and taking personal belong-ings; (b) verbal bullying, which includes threats and malicious teasing; and (c) psychological bullying, which includes spreading rumors and social manipulation. Research in this area was spearheaded by Olweus (1993) in Scandinavia who found a strong relationship between experiencing bullying in youth and later criminal behavior. Recent interest in bullying in the United States has increased as it has been proposed as a risk factor for targeted violence. The U.S. Surgeon General's report (2001) notes that Olweus's *Bullying Prevention Program* is effective in reducing bullying and antisocial behavior. However, bullying is not addressed by the U.S. Surgeon General as a risk factor except in noting that it is very situational. The impact of bullying for the school setting is especially relevant due to the pervasiveness of the problem. Estimates range from 17 percent (Ericson 2001) to 30 percent (Nansel et al. 2001). Espelage, Bosworth, and Simon (2000) reported that only 19 percent of a sample of 558 adolescents engaged in no bullying behavior for the previous month per their self-report. This latter study focused more on assessing specific bullying behaviors (i.e., teasing or threatening) rather than on identification of a more characterological "bully." Given the high rate of reported bullying behavior, the authors recommend that bullying be viewed as a continuum of behavior for all students. It appears reasonable but somewhat circular to conclude that bullying has a strong relationship to aggression, but further research is needed to clarify how well bullying predicts later violence.

Other Individual Risk Factors

Psychological condition, which includes variables related to attention deficit hyperactivity disorder (ADHD), and more general descriptors such as psychopathology were relatively small but significant predictors of later violence for young children and adolescents (Lipsey and Derzon 1998). Hawkins et al. (1998) reported that hyperactivity or attention deficits in childhood (age 10) or adolescence doubled the risk of violent behavior by age 18. The latter authors also reported that sensation-seeking behavior in adolescence doubled the risk for later violence.

FAMILY

Low socioeconomic status/poverty is a significant risk factor, more for younger children than adolescents, per the Lipsey and Derzon (1998) study.

The pervasive effects of poverty on multiple indicators of physical, mental, and behavioral health are well documented (Payne 2002). Poor families are more likely to be exposed to other major risk factors such as drugs and gangs, and less likely to have the resources to develop protective factors, which might prevent later violence. Having antisocial parents is another risk factor that is stronger for young children than adolescents, although Hawkins et al. (1998) noted that parent criminality at age 19 doubled the risk for violence at age 18. Hawkins et al. also found that when parents of 10-year-old children had favorable attributes towards violence, it doubled the risk for later violence. Poor parenting variables take on a more pronounced role as risk factors for adolescents as compared with younger children. Poor family management practices at age 14 and 16 doubled the risk for later violence. Family conflict and residential mobility at age 16 also doubled the risk for violence at age 18 (Hawkins et al. 1998). However, in general, family risk factors decrease as children reach adolescence, whereas peer influences take on heightened importance.

PEER GROUP RISK FACTORS

Weak Social Ties/Antisocial Peers

This risk factor had the highest effect size (.39) in the Lipsey and Derzon (1998) study. All three peer group risk factors identified in table 2.1 have a much more pronounced effect for adolescents than for younger children. Experiencing significant adolescent rejection is related to multiple problems involving delinquency and aggression (Borum 2000). Youths who share the experiences and consequences of peer problems may gravitate towards one another and form antisocial peer groups. However, it is important to note that these two risk factors have significant effects independent of each other (U.S. Surgeon General 2001).

Gangs

Along with the crack cocaine epidemic and easy access to firearms, gang activity and violence were among the prime causes of the sharp increase in youth violence from 1983 to 1994 (U.S. Surgeon General 2001). Re-

Table 2.1. Predictors for Later Violence or Serious Delinquency

Domain	Predictors Occurring at age 6–11	Predictors Occurring at age 12–14
	General Offenses	General offenses
Individual	Substance use	Psychological condition
	Being male	Hyperactivity/Attention deficits
	Aggression**	Sensation seeking
	Psychological condition	Restlessness
	Hyperactivity/Attention Deficits	Difficulty concentrating**
	Problem (antisocial) behavior	Risk taking
	Exposure to television violence	Aggression**
	Medical, physical	Being male
	Low IQ	Physical violence
	Antisocial attitudes, beliefs	Drug Selling
	Dishonesty**	Antisocial attitudes, beliefs
		Crimes against persons
		Problem (antisocial) behavior
		Low IQ
		Substance use
Family	Low socioeconomic status/poverty	Poor parent-child relations
	Antisocial parents	Harsh, lax discipline; poor monitoring, supervision
	Parental attitudes towards violence	Low parental involvement
	Poor parent-child relations	Antisocial parents
	Harsh, lax, or inconsistent discipline	Broken home
	Broken home	Low socioeconomic status/poverty
	Separation from parents	Abusive parents
	Other family conditions	Other family conditions
	Abusive parents	Family conflict**
	Neglect	Residential mobility
Community		Neighborhood crime, drugs
		Neighborhood disorganization
		Knowing criminal adults
		Drug availability
Peer Group	Weak social ties	Weak social ties
	Antisocial peers	Antisocial, delinquent peers
		Gang membership
School	Poor attitude, performance	Poor attitude, performance
	Behavior problems	Academic failure
		Low commitment to schooling
		Low educational aspirations
		Multiple school transitions

** Males only (U.S. Surgeon General 2001)

cent data suggest that the number of youth gangs has decreased from 1996 to 2000 (Egley 2002). However, the same report notes that the number of gangs and gang members in large cities (more than 250,000) did not significantly change during that time period, with roughly half of these cities experiencing an increase in gang-related homicides for 1999–2000. Like substance use, gangs are a major risk factor that is still quite present despite the recent decline in overall youth violence. Gang members are more likely to be male and African American or Hispanic (Snyder and Sickmund 1999). Disorganized communities (high crime, drugs, gangs, poor housing, physical deterioration, and dense living conditions) are at risk for gang presence (Williams and Van Dorn 1999). In his review, Thornberry (1998) emphasized the strong connection between gang involvement and a disproportionately high rate of serious violent behavior. Hawkins et al. (1998) noted that youths who belonged to a gang at 14 years of age were three times more likely to experience violence at 18 years of age, while those who belonged to a gang at 16 years of age were four times more likely to engage in later violence. Last, it is important to note that gang membership is a distinct risk factor apart from simply having an antisocial or delinquent peer group (Thornberry 1998).

Community Risk Factors

Urban communities considered at risk have been characterized as socially disorganized, meaning that they have low socioeconomic status, high residential turnover, and social/ethnic heterogeneity, all of which saps their resources and sense of community (Laub and Lauritsen 1998). Social disorganization at the neighborhood level and neighborhood crime in general have been identified as small predictors of later violence for 12–14-year-olds (U.S. Surgeon General 2001). Hawkins et al. (1998) also found that drug availability and knowing criminal adults increased the risk for later violence for 14–16-year-olds. High housing density has been associated with higher rates of violence (Laub and Lauritsen 1998) although it is not recognized as a major risk factor by itself. With regards to younger children, community risk factors appear to be mediated by more direct risk factors or protective factors, and therefore do not have direct effects on later violence by themselves (U.S. Surgeon General 2001).

Weapons

Since the youth violence epidemic of the 1980s and early 1990s, examining weapons as a risk factor usually means looking at firearms rather than other weapons. Firearms are so strongly associated with youth violence that they are often omitted from reviews of risk factors and instead conceptualized as a violent act (i.e., firearm use or possession) in and of themselves. Neither the U.S. Surgeon General's Report (2001), Lipsey and Derzon, (1998) nor Hawkins et al. (1998) examines firearms as a specific risk factor, due to methodological reasons rather than a deemphasis of this variable. While there are many studies that examine the "how" of firearms and youth violence, far fewer examine the "why" connection. Firearm possession is often considered to be a situational variable (U.S. Surgeon General 2001) and therefore difficult to track in the same manner as risk factors such as substance use or gang affiliation. However, in a real-life situation involving a threat assessment (Borum 2000) or risk assessment (Ryan-Arrendondo et al. 2001), assessing access/availability of firearms is of primary importance.

Many of the other areas of risk assessment examine traditional risk factors such as history of aggression, academic performance, and substance use. Mercy and Rosenberg (1998) concluded that there is little doubt that the presence of firearms has greatly increased the lethality of interpersonal youth violence. One can only conjecture how many homicides would have been survivable stab wounds or concussions if firearms were not so prevalent. On the other hand, one can look at the many Western societies that have lower youth violence and youth homicide rates than the United States. Researchers in these countries do not report on absence of significant youth violence, but they do emphasize the lack of firearm use as a main difference when compared with the United States (Harel 1999). The implication is that if Western European nations were as equally saturated with firearms as the United States, those countries would have similar youth violence patterns as the United States.

Firearm possession, drug dealing, and gang affiliation are three frequently co-occurring risk factors that account for a high proportion of violent acts among youth (U.S. Surgeon General 2001). Residing in an urban area increases access to firearms; however, little research has examined the correlates of firearm possession among suburban and rural youth (Mercy and Rosenberg 1998). Several reviews (Howard and Jensen 1999; Mercy and Rosenberg 1998; Page and Hammermeister 1997) note that research does not support the idea that youths carry firearms for purely defensive or protective reasons. Instead, gun carrying is more directly related to aggressive, antisocial, and delinquent patterns of thought and behavior. Page and Hammermeister (1997) suggested that preventative measures might be more productive when directed toward these latter risk factors, rather than toward firearm possession.

School Violence Risk Factors

Given that the focus of this book is on school violence, rather than youth violence, two important points are worth stressing as a backdrop for considering this topic. First, the schools have been and continue to be one of the safest places for children and adolescents. Most acts of serious violence happen in places other than school buildings during the school day. Second, as Furlong and Morrison (2000) have articulated, school violence is better conceptualized as complex than simply violence that occurs at school. Rather, the school is a *system* with inherently blurred boundaries between acts of aggression (i.e., name-calling, shoving) versus acts of violence. Moreover, it would be equally artificial to overly separate this school system from the family and community systems within which they interact. Schools are strongly identified by their surrounding communities and vice versa, creating a shared responsibility for successes and problems. Family units of all types also have a reciprocal and strongly interwoven relationship with the schools. For example, parents often look to the schools for services that go well beyond basic education, such as social development, athletic training, and identification of emotional/ behavioral problems. For most students, the school functions as their primary hub in which to experience multiple social and emotional challenges, including violence. Major risk factors for violence, such as gangs, substance use, and guns, take on different meanings in the school context. For example, school gangs are less violent and lethal than criminal street gangs (Laub and Lauritsen 1998).

Other risk factors, such as bullying, are most easily conceptualized within the school setting. Many of these challenges may have their origins in the family or community, but for the child they are played out within the school. An example of this would be a youth with antisocial, substance-abusing parents, who fails in school partly due to his own substance use. Such a scenario might come under antisocial parents (family domain), academic failure (school domain), or substance use (individual domain). For a school-age child or adolescent it is unlikely that the school setting would not be involved or affected in some way. Even an underage gang member who has dropped out of school and is working the streets might be selling drugs or recruiting peers still in school.

For 6–11-year-olds, the only risk factor identified in the Lipsey and Derzon (1998) meta-analysis was having a poor school attitude and performance, which was in the lower range of effect sizes for that age group. Hawkins et al. (1998) found that school behavior problems at age 10 significantly predicted later violence at age 18. For 12–14-year-olds, poor school attitude or poor school performance (academic failure) are mildly predictive of later violence (Lipsey and Derzon 1998). In the Hawkins et al. (1998) study, low academic performance at 10, 14, and 16 years of age predicted increased violence risk at age 18. The latter study also noted that low educational commitment, low aspirations, and multiple school transitions at 14 and 16 years of age significantly predicted an increased risk for violence at age 18.

Other aspects of risk for school violence have more to do with contextual rather than the individual-type factors just mentioned. A recent review by Werner, Weisst, and Krulak (1999) identified several such variables, including location of violence within the school itself and degree of overcrowdedness within the school. Incidents of violence are greater in urban schools compared with suburban or rural settings, but the magnitude of this difference may be small (Furlong and Morrison 2000). School violence tends to occur in settings with minimal supervision and structured activities, such as hallways, buses, bathrooms, and some classrooms (Werner et al. 1999). Larger schools tend to have more violence. Similarly, schools with overcrowded classrooms are at higher risk. With school homicides specifically, the beginning of each semester appears to be more associated with violent deaths (Centers for Disease Control 2001). Huizinga and Jakob-Chien (1998) noted that truancy and suspensions were more associated with serious offending than were grades or dropping out of school. Morrison and Skiba (2001) articulate the risks and limitations of using school suspensions to identify potentially violent students, noting that many suspensions are for offenses far less serious than overt violence.

CONCLUSION

Although no single or multiple causes for youth and school violence have been identified, researchers have identified several risk factors that put children and adolescents "at risk" for violent behavior. This chapter provided an overview of individual, family, peer group, community, and school risk factors. It is important for educators to be aware of these risk factors when considering prevention and intervention strategies that help reduce the risk factors. More rigorous research designs and methodology will be needed in determining the effectiveness of the interventions addressing risk factors. In addition, prevention and intervention research is needed that would be practical for educators and other interested parties to implement, which would reduce or eliminate youth violence or risk factors for violence.

REFERENCES

Acosta, O. M., K. E. Albus, M. W. Reynolds, D. Spriggs, and M. D. Weist. 2001. Assessing the status of research on violence-related problems among youth. *Journal of Clinical Child Psychology* 30: 152–60.

American Psychological Association. 1993. *Violence and youth: Psychology's response. Volume I: Summary report of the American Psychological Association commission on violence and youth.* Washington, D.C.: Author.

Anderson, C. A., and K. E. Dill. 2000. Video games and aggressive thoughts, feelings, and behavior in the laboratory and in life. *Journal of Personality and Social Psychology* 78: 772–90.

Bensley, L., and J. Van Eenuyk. 2001. Video games and real-life aggression: Review of the literature. *Journal of Adolescent Health* 29: 244–57.

Borum, R. 2000. Assessing violence risk among youth. *Journal of Clinical Psychology* 56(10): 1263–289.

Budnick, K. J., and Shields-Fletcher, E. 1998, September. What about girls? *OJJDP* Fact Sheet, 84. Washington, D.C.: U.S. Department of Justice, Office of Juvenile Justice and Delinquency Preventions.

Centers for Disease Control. 2001. *Temporal variations in school-associated student homicide and suicide events—United States, 1992–1999.* Morbidity and Mortality Weekly Report, 50. 31: 657–61.

Crick, N. D., and Grotpeter, J. K. 1995. Relational aggression, gender, and social-psychological adjustment. *Child Development* 66: 710–22.

Derzon, J. H. (2001). Antisocial behavior and the prediction of violence: A meta-analysis. *Psychology in the Schools* 38: 93–106.

Dwyer, K. P., and D. Osher. 2000. Safeguarding our children: An action guide. Implementing early warning, timely responses. *Exceptional Children* 66(3): 347–66.

Egley, A. 2002. *National youth gang survey trends from 1996 to 2000.* Office of Juvenile Justice and Delinquency Prevention, Fact Sheet No. 3. Washington, D.C.: Department of Justice.

Ericson, N. 2001. *Addressing the problem of juvenile bullying.* Office of Juvenile Justice and Delinquency Prevention, Fact Sheet No. 27. Washington, D.C.: Department of Justice.

Espelage, D. L., K. Bosworth, and T. R. Simon. 2000. Examining the social context of bullying behaviors in early adolescence. *Journal of Counseling and Development* 78: 326–33.

Furlong, M., and G. Morrison. 2000. The school in school violence: Definitions and facts. *Journal of Emotional and Behavioral Disorders* 8(2): 71–81.

Harel, Y. 1999. A cross-national study of youth violence in Europe. *International Journal of Adolescent Medicine and Health* 11: 121–34.

Hawkins, J. D., T. L. Herrenkohl, D. P. Farrington, D. Brewer, R. F. Catalano, and T. W. Harachi. 1998. A review of predictors of youth violence. In *Serious and violent juvenile offenders: Risk factors and successful interventions,* ed. R. Loeber and D. P. Farrington, pp. 106–46. Thousand Oaks, Calif.: Sage.

Howard, M. O., and J. M. Jenson. 1999. Causes of youth violence. In *Youth Violence: Current Research and Recent Practice Innovations,* ed. J. M. Jenson and M. O. Howard, pp. 19–42. Washington, D.C.: NASW Press.

Huizinga, D., and C. Jokob-Chien. 1998. Contemporaneous co-occurrence of serious and violent juvenile offending and other problem behaviors. In *Serious and violent juvenile offenders: Risk factors and successful interventions,* ed. R. Loeber and D. P. Farrington, pp. 46–67. Thousand Oaks, Calif.: Sage.

Kazdin, A. E. 1995. *Conduct disorders in childhood & adolescence* (2nd ed.). Thousand Oaks, CA: Sage.

Laub, J. H., and J. L. Lauritsen. 1998. The interdependence of school violence with neighborhood and family conditions. In *Violence in American schools: A new perspective,* ed. D. S. Elliott, B. A. Hamburg, and K. R. Williams, pp. 127–55. New York: Cambridge University Press.

Leschied, A. W., Cummings, A. L., Van Brunschot, M., Cunningham, A., and Saunders, A. 2001. Aggression in adolescent girls: Implications for policy, prevention, and treatment. *Canadian Psychology*, 42(3): 200–215.

Lipsey, M. W., and J. H. Derzon. 1998. Predictors of violent and serious delinquency in adolescence and early adulthood: A synthesis of longitudinal research. In *Serious and violent juvenile offenders: Risk factors and successful interventions,* ed. R. Loeber and D. P. Farrington, pp. 86–105. Thousand Oaks, Calif.: Sage.

Loeber, R., and M. Stouthamer-Loeber. 1998. Juvenile aggression at home and school. In *Violence in american schools: a new perspective,* eds. D.S. Elliot, B. A. Hamburg, and K. R. Williams, pp. 94–126. New York: Cambridge University Press.

Mercy, J., and M. L. Rosenberg. 1998. Preventing firearm violence in and around schools. In *Violence in american schools: a new perspective,* eds. D.S. Elliot, B. A. Hamburg, and K. R. Williams, pp. 159–87. New York: Cambridge University Press.

Mifflin, L. 1999, May 9. Many researchers say link is already clear on media and youth violence. *New York Times*, A21.

Mitchell, S., and Rosa, P. 1979. Boyhood behavior problems as precursors of criminality: A fifteen-year follow-up study. *Journal of Child Psychology and Psychiatry* 22: 19–33.

Moran, J. R., and J. M. Jenson. 1999. Adolescent substance abuse and youth violence. In *Youth violence: Current research and recent practice innovations,* ed. J. M. Jenson and M. O. Howard, pp. 173–98. Washington D.C.: NASW Press.

Morrison, G. M., and R. Skiba. 2001. Predicting violence from school misbehavior: Promises and perils. *Psychology in Schools* 38(2): 173–84.

Nansel, T. R., M. Overpeck, R. S. Pilla, W. J. Ruan, B. Simons-Morton, and P. Scheidt. 2001. Bullying behaviors among U.S. youth: Prevalence and association with psychosocial adjustment. *Journal of the American Medical Association* 285(16): 2094–100.

Olweus, D. 1993. Bully/victim problems among schoolchildren: Long-term consequences and an effective intervention program. In *Mental disorder and crime*, ed. S. Hodgins, pp. 317–49. Thousand Oaks, Calif.: Sage.

Page, R. M., and J. Hammermeister. 1997. Weapon-carrying and youth violence. *Adolescence* 32: 505–14.

Paik, H., and G. Comstock. 1994. The effects of television violence on antisocial behavior: A meta-analysis. *Communication Research* 21: 516–46.

Payne, J. L. 2002. Violence in the twentieth century. *Independent Review* 6(3): 447–49.

Potter, C. C. 1999. Violence and aggression in girls. In *Youth Violence: Current research and practice innovations*, ed. J. M. Jensen and M. O. Howard, pp. 113–37. Washington, D.C.: NASA.

Ryan-Arrendondo, K., K. L. Renouf, C. Egyed, M. Docey, M. Dobbins, S. Sanchez, and B. Rakowitz. 2001. Threats of violence in schools: The Dallas independent school district's response. *Psychology in the Schools* 38: 185–96.

Smith, S. L., and Donnerstein, E. 1998. Media violence. In *Human aggression: Theories, research, and implications for social policy*, ed. R. E. Geen and E. Donnerstein, pp. 139–65. San Diego: Academic Press.

Snyder, H. N., and M. Sickmund. 1999. *Juvenile offenders and victims: 1999 national report* (NCJ 178257). Washington, D.C.: U.S. Department of Justice.

Thornberry, T. P. (1998). Membership in youth gangs and involvement in serious, violent offending. In *Serious and violent juvenile offenders: Risk factors and successful interventions*, eds. R. Loeber and D. P. Farrington. Thousand Oaks, Calif.: Sage.

U.S. Surgeon General. 2001. *Youth violence: A report of the U.S. Surgeon General*. Washington, D.C.: U.S. Surgeon General Office, http://surgeongeneral. gov.library/youthviolence/toc.html

Werner, B. S., M. D. Weisst, and A. Krulak. 1999. Risk factors for school violence. *Urban Education* 34: 52–69.

Williams, J. H., and Van Dorn, R. 1999. Delinquency, gangs, and youth violence. In *Youth violence: Current research and practice innovations*, ed. J. M. Jensen and M. O. Howard, pp. 198–215. Washington, D.C.: NASW Press.

Chapter Three

Are Children with Special Needs Committing School Violence?

Denise Smith

The random acts of targeted school shootings of the past several years have prompted many scholars to search for explanations of *why* and question *who* is committing these horrific violent acts and whether additional attacks will occur. In fact, the U.S. Secret Service (2002) examined the thinking, planning, and other preattack behaviors engaged by attackers who carried out the school shootings to determine (a) whether the attacks were being planned, and, (b) if yes, what could have been done to prevent further attacks. The major findings reported were as follows:

- Incidents of targeted violence at school rarely were sudden, impulsive acts.
- Prior to most incidents, other people knew about the attacker's idea or plan to attack.
- There is no useful "profile" of students engaged in targeted school violence.
- Most attackers engaged in some behavior prior to the incident that caused others concern or indicated a need for help.
- Most attackers had difficulty coping with significant losses or personal failures. Moreover, many had conspired or attempted suicide.
- Many attackers felt bullied, persecuted, or injured by others prior to the attack.
- Most attackers had access to and had weapons prior to the attack.
- In many cases, other students were involved in some capacity.
- Despite prompt law enforcement responses, most shooting incidents were stopped by means other than law enforcement intervention.

Other researchers have questioned the role, if any, children with disabilities played in any of the recent school-yard shootings (Barr and Parrett 2001; Bender, Shubert, and McLaughlin 2001; Shubert et al. 1999) while others have considered the role special education legislation has played in school violence (Cahir 2000; Rudo, Robbins, and Smith 2002). This chapter provides an overview of special education legislation and its role in school violence, followed by a discussion of children with disabilities and their involvement with juvenile delinquency, ending with a discussion of what role, if any, special education should play as a prevention measure for school violence.

SPECIAL EDUCATION LEGISLATION AND SCHOOL VIOLENCE

Approximately 11 percent of school-age children between the ages of 6 and 17 are identified as receiving special education services in the United States (U.S. Department of Education 1998). Public Law 105-17, the Individuals with Disabilities Act (IDEA), which is the reauthorization of P.L. 94-142 Education for All Handicapped Children Act, protects the educational interests of children with disabilities. Some believe that P.L. 105-17 prevents school violence (Rudo et al. 2002) whereas others believe that it promotes school violence (Cahir 2000).

According to IDEA, special education is "specifically designed instruction, at no cost to parents, to meet the unique needs of a child with a disability. . . . This includes instruction conducted in the classroom, home, hospitals and institutions, and in other settings and instruction in physical education" (Indiana Department of Education 2000, 13). Two major provisions of IDEA includes the right to free and appropriate education with nondisabled peers to the maximum extent appropriate or what has been referred to as the *least restrictive environment.* The key to providing a free and appropriate education is individualized instruction. To ensure that all children identified as having a disability receive individualized instruction, IDEA mandates that an individualized education program (IEP) be developed. In the development of this individualized program, the case conference committee considers the child's current level of educational performance and special needs, the services to be delivered, objectives to be met, timelines for completion, and assessment progress.

Perhaps the most controversial aspects of Public Law 105-17 are the discipline provisions, such as the "stay-put" rule and the cumulative ten-school-day limit on suspensions. Legislation mandates that a child with a disability remain in his or her current educational placement, pending the completion of any due-process proceedings, court proceedings, or appeals. Many argue that the stay-put provision of IDEA promotes school violence because it unfairly protects students with disabilities who are disruptive or violent. They argue that the school's options are limited when there is a legitimate reason to remove a dangerous or extremely disruptive child.

Some school administrators and many members of Congress thought that the stay-put provision contributed to the excessive violence that has erupted in the schools during the past several years (Trump 1999). For example, Congress was concerned that students with disabilities could bring guns to school and yet would not be expelled as would their nondisabled violent peers. Furthermore, it was believed that IDEA prevented school officials from disciplining and expelling students with disabilities with behavior problems "even if a student with a disability commits a serious infraction of the rules, such as bringing a gun to school, he or she can only be suspended for 10 days as opposed to the mandatory one year expulsion handed to other students accused of the same crime" (Cahir 2000, 75). According to Cahir "many school officials argue that IDEA creates a dangerous Catch 22. If a student's violent or antisocial behavior stems from a disability, the officials' disciplinary options become limited. Only when a child's education team determines that his misconduct is unrelated to his disability may the school discipline the student as it would others" (Cahir 2000, 75).

Cahir argues that students with a disability charged with weapons and drug-related offenses can be removed from their school and sent to an alternative placement for a maximum of forty-five calendar days. This, according to Cahir, is in direct contrast to the 1994 federal Gun-Free Schools Act, which requires that any nondisabled child who possesses a gun in school be expelled for at least one year. "Schools can also move a child with a disability to an alternative placement if a hearing officer determines the student poses a threat to himself or others—a litigious, appealable, time-consuming process" (Cahir 2000, 75).

Moreover, some school administrators and teachers raised concerns about their ability to maintain school safety and order and at the same time instruct students with disabilities. It was argued that when students with

disabilities engaged in serious misconduct, they continued to receive educational services in schools because of the protections afforded by
IDEA. In contrast, nondisabled students involved in similar misconduct
were suspended or expelled without educational services (U.S. General
Accounting Office 2001).

In contrast, others believe that IDEA attempts to strike a balance
between the need to provide a safe, orderly environment and the need to
protect children with disabilities from unwarranted exclusion through disciplinary proceedings (Burrell and Warboys 2000; Rudo et al. 2002). To
appreciate this controversy one must understand the intent of IDEA's stay-
put provision and other provisions provided by special education legislation.

School personnel may suspend children with disabilities for up to ten
school days at a time for separate incidents of misconduct to the extent
that such action would be applied to nondisabled peers. Change in placement for more than ten consecutive school days constitutes a change in
educational placement, which triggers several procedural safeguards. The
IEP team must meet immediately to review the relationship between
the child's disability and the behavior subject to disciplinary action. The
IEP team takes into consideration several factors such as evaluation and
diagnostic results, placement appropriateness, if the disability impaired
the child's ability to understand the consequences of the behavior subject
to discipline, and if the child's disability impaired his ability to control the
behavior.

If the behavior was a result of the child's disability, the IEP team revis-
its the individualized program to determine what changes need to be implemented to address the child's behavior. Rudo et al. (2002) believe that
the IEP is one way to decrease a child's violent behavior, especially since
IDEA requires educators to conduct functional behavioral assessments
and to implement behavior intervention plans that include positive
behavioral interventions and supports. These mandates are aimed at providing students with disabilities, particularly those who are at risk for or
who engage in aggressive and violent behavior, with the necessary skills
to handle their anger and aggression in acceptable ways.

On the other hand, if the IEP team determines that the violent behavior
was not a manifestation of the child's disability then disciplinary procedures used for nondisabled peers can be used with the child with a dis-

ability. On May 20, 1999, the Senate approved an amendment to Juvenile Justice Bill that changes the IDEA stay-put rule. This revision gives school officials the option of removing for one year a student with a disability who brings a bomb or gun to school. This revision contradicts the assumption that IDEA promotes school violence. In essence, IDEA acknowledges the importance of addressing behavioral problems for children with special needs and requires special educators to address identified behavioral problems.

The U.S. General Accounting Office (GAO) (2001) conducted a study to determine how the IDEA amendments of 1997 affected the ability of schools to maintain a safe environment conducive to learning. The results suggest that nondisabled students and students with disabilities are generally disciplined the same, for example, 60 percent to 65 percent of students with or without disabilities who engage in misconduct are given out-of-school suspension. The length of suspension is about the same and less than half of the suspended students with or without disabilities receive educational services during their suspensions. It seems that the argument that IDEA promotes violence is unfounded; in fact, principals interviewed during the GAO study indicated that IDEA plays a limited role in affecting schools ability to properly discipline students.

ARE CHILDREN WITH DISABILITIES COMMITTING VIOLENT ACTS IN SCHOOL?

Students with disabilities who are considered at potential risk for committing violent acts in school include children with learning disabilities, emotional disabilities, and attention deficit hyperactivity disorder (ADHD). Table 3.1 provides the IDEA definition of students with learning and emotional disabilities. Table 3.2 provides the Diagnostic Statistical Manual (DSM–IV) criteria for ADHD.

According to Burrell and Warboys (2000), "disabilities that are frequently encountered among delinquents include emotional disturbance, specific learning disabilities, mental retardation, other health impairments (such as ADHD), and speech or language impairment" (2). The two most common disabilities found in the juvenile justice system are specific learning disabilities and emotional disturbance (Burrell and Warboys 2000).

Table 3.1.   Definitions of Children with Learning and Emotional Disabilities

Disability	Definition
Learning Disabilities	A disorder in one or more of the basic psychological processes involved in understanding or in using language, spoken or written, that may manifest itself in an imperfect ability to listen, speak, read, write, spell or do mathematical calculations. It may include conditions such as perceptual disabilities, brain injury, minimal brain dysfunction, dyslexia, and developmental aphasia but not a learning problem that is primarily the result of environmental, cultural, or economic disadvantage
Emotional Disturbance	Condition exhibiting one or more of the following characteristics over a long period of time and to a marked degree that adversely affects a child's educational performance:

1. an inability to learn that cannot be explained by intellectual, sensory, or health factors
2. an inability to build or maintain satisfactory interpersonal relationships with peers and teachers
3. inappropriate types of behaviors or feelings under normal circumstances
4. a general pervasive mood of unhappiness or depression
5. a tendency to develop physical symptoms or fears associated with personal or school problems

The term includes schizophrenia. The term does not apply to children who are socially maladjusted, unless it is determined that they have an emotional disturbance

SRI International conducted a National Longitudinal Transition Study from 1987 to 1993 and found that arrest rates increased over time among youth with disabilities, from 19 percent when they had been out of secondary school up to two years to 30 percent three years later. Furthermore, arrest rates were highest and increased most dramatically for youth with serious emotional disturbances. Two years out of high school, 37 percent had been arrested. By the time youth with disabilities had been out of school three to five years, 58 percent had been arrested at some time. Arrest rates also were relatively high for youth with learning disabilities (31 percent had been arrested three to five years after high school). Arrest rates were less than 20 percent for most other disability categories and less than 10 percent for youth with orthopedic and other health impairments and youth who were deaf/blind. The arrest rate three to five years after secondary school was 56 percent among high school dropouts, compared

Table 3.2.   Definition of Attention Deficit Hyperactivity Disorder (ADHD)

A. Either (1) or (2):

    1. six (or more) of the following symptoms of inattention have persisted for at least 6 months to a degree that is maladaptive and inconsistent with developmental level:

        a. often fails to give close attention to details or makes careless mistakes in schoolwork, work, or other activities

        b. often has difficulty sustaining attention in tasks or play activities

        c. often does not seem to listen when spoken to directly

        d. often does not follow through on instructions and fails to finish schoolwork, chores, or duties in the workplace (not due to oppositional behavior or failure to understand instructions)

        e. often has difficulty organizing tasks and activities

        f. often avoids, dislikes, or is reluctant to engage in tasks that require sustained mental effort (such as schoolwork or homework)

        g. often loses things necessary for tasks or activities (e.g., toys, school assignments, pencils, books, or tools)

        h. is often easily distracted by extraneous stimuli

        i. is often forgetful in daily activities

    2. six (or more) of the following symptoms of hyperactivity-impulsivity have persisted for at least 6 months to a degree that is maladaptive and inconsistent with developmental level:

    Hyperactivity

        a. often fidgets with hands or feet or squirms in seat

        b. often leaves seat in classroom or in other situations in which remaining seated is expected

        c. often runs about or climbs excessively in situations in which it is inappropriate (in adolescents or adults, may be limited to subjective feelings of restlessness)

        d. often has difficulty playing or engaging in leisure activities quietly

        e. is often "on the go" or often acts as if "driven by a motor" often talks excessively

    Impulsivity

        f. often blurts out answers before questions have been completed

        g. often has difficulty awaiting turn

        h. often interrupts or intrudes on others (e.g., butts into conversations or games)

B. Some hyperactive-impulsive or inattentive symptoms that caused impairment were present before age 7 years.

C. Some impairment from the symptoms is present in two or more settings (e.g., at school [or work] and at home).

D. There must be clear evidence of clinically significant impairment in social, academic, or occupational functioning.

E. The symptoms do not occur exclusively during the course of a Pervasive Developmental Disorder, Schizophrenia, or other Psychotic Disorder and are not

(continued)

Table 3.2.   Definition of Attention Deficit Hyperactivity Disorder (ADHD) *(continued)*

better accounted for by another mental disorder (e.g., Mood Disorder, Anxiety Disorder, Dissociative Disorder, or a Personality Disorder).

Specify Type:

- Attention-Deficit/Hyperactivity Disorder, Combined Type: if both Criteria A1 and A2 are met for the past 6 months
- Attention-Deficit/Hyperactivity Disorder, Predominantly Inattentive Type: if Criterion A1 is met but Criterion A2 is not met for the past 6 months

Attention-Deficit/Hyperactivity Disorder, Predominantly Hyperactive-Impulsive Type: if Criterion A2 is met but Criterion A1 is not met for the past 6 months

with 16 percent among graduates and 10 percent among those who aged out of school. Among dropouts with serious emotional disturbances, the arrest rate was 73 percent.

CHILDREN WITH EMOTIONAL DISTURBANCE AND JUVENILE DELINQUENCY

The relationship between emotional or behavioral disorders and serious juvenile problems is strong. The potential for serious juvenile problems is clear in young boys and girls (Day and Hunt 1996; Miller-Johnson et al. 1999; Walker and Sylvester 1994):

- Problem behaviors are clearly established by ages 4 to 5.
- Overt (e.g., bullying) and covert (e.g., stealing) antisocial activities are becoming behavior patterns.
- Problems happen across settings (home, school, community).
- The child is both overactive and inattentive.
- Extreme aggression is frequent.

Of these five characteristics of young children prone to later problems, the single best predictor is aggression. For example, 6th graders referred to special education because of both violent and nonviolent inappropriate behaviors are likely to present chronic discipline problems during their remaining school years (Tobin and Sugai 1999). The strong relationship between emotional disturbance and juvenile delinquency has served as a catalyst for some researchers to question the common factors of the school shootings and characteristics of students with emotional disturbance. Shubert et al. (1999) examined the school-yard shootings that occurred from October 1997 to May 1998 in Pearl, Mississippi; West Paducah, Kentucky; Jonesborough, Arkansas; Edinboro, Pennsylvania; and Springfield, Oregon, to determine common factors among the violent young perpetrators. One common factor noted was that although no one was identified as having a disability, "each demonstrated some indicators to peers of fairly serious emotional problems" (1).

After subsequent school-yard shootings in Littleton, Colorado, and Conyers, Georgia, Bender et al. (2001) analyzed the shootings to determine common factors of the violent perpetrators. When comparing Shubert et al.'s analysis with Bender et al.'s analysis, similar findings were noted. For example, Bender et al. noted that "each of the students responsible for the shootings demonstrated some type of emotional trouble" (2).

LEARNING DISABILITIES AND DELINQUENCY

The link between learning disabilities and delinquency is not clear. Early research studies suggested that students with learning disabilities (LD) were at greater risk for delinquency than their nondisabled peers (Broder et al. 1981; Keiltz and Dunivant 1986; Satterfield, Hoppe, and Schell 1982). In fact, three hypotheses were posed as the causal explanations for the link between LD and delinquency. The first hypothesis, school failure, suggests that students with LD experience academic failure, which leads to the development of a negative self-image, which in turn leads to school dropout and delinquency. A second hypothesis is the differential treatment hypothesis, which postulates that students with LD engage in delinquent acts at the same rates as nondisabled peers but are more likely to be arrested or adjudicated. The third hypothesis, the susceptibility hypothesis, proposes that children with LD frequently have "a variety of troublesome personality characteristics" (see Murray 1976 for a comprehensive discussion of these three hypotheses).

Despite reports that students with learning disabilities are frequently among juvenile delinquents (Burrell and Warboys 2000), and a number of professionals have speculated that learning disabilities contribute to the increased risk for delinquent behavior, empirical data supporting a causal relationship does not exist. In fact, recent research suggests that there is no relationship between LD and delinquency. Malmgren, Abbott, and Hawkins (1999) examined longitudinal data from a seven-year prospective study to determine whether the presence of LD increased a youth's risk for becoming a juvenile delinquent. The results did not confirm a direct relationship between LD and delinquency. The authors also suggest that findings of positive correlation noted in earlier studies may have been due to confounding variables such as LD and age, LD and ethnicity, and LD and socioeconomic status.

Neurological Impairment

Although recent research findings suggest that there is no correlation between LD and delinquency, some researchers have examined the relationship between neurological impairment and violence. Neuroimaging research studies such as positron emission tomography (PET), single photon emission computed tomography (SPECT), and functional magnetic resonance imaging (fMRI) have been conducted to examine violence and aggression. For example, Volkow et al. (1995) and Raine et al. (1998) used PET scans to determine that decreased glucose metabolism in the prefrontal and medial temporal cortex was associated with increased aggressive behaviors in adults.

Amen (1996) conducted brain studies using SPECT and found that adolescents and adults with aggressiveness showed abnormalities of cerebral blood flow in the frontal and temporal lobes. Using fMRI, Rubia et al. (1999) found abnormal frontal lobe function in adolescents; similar findings were noted in Bush et al.'s (1999) study of adults with attention deficit disorder. Most recently, Matthews (2002) found that when children diagnosed with oppositional defiant disorder or conduct disorder were exposed to media violence, they demonstrated less activation in the frontal lobe. Brower and Price (2001) examined the link between frontal lobe dysfunction and violent and criminal behavior. They concluded that clinically significant frontal lobe dysfunction is associated with aggressive behavior, with impulsivity having the strongest relationship. Furthermore, they found that no study had reliably demonstrated a characteristic pattern of frontal network dysfunction predictive of violent crime. However, Flannery (1999) and Weinberger (2002) postulate that brain development can contribute to school violence. Weinberger believes that "school shootings occur because the prefrontal cortex in a teenage brain is not fully developed." The prefrontal cortex is part of the brain that enables people to act rationally and resist violent impulses. However, the cortex is not fully functional until adulthood. Consequently, it is believed that adolescents responsible for school shootings are unable to control their impulses and are unaware of the long-range consequences of their actions. Neurodevelopment research has also focused on the possibility that abuse and neglect, particularly during infancy and early childhood, may negatively affect brain development because of either physical injury or neurochemical alterations in response to trauma (Perry 1997). Altered neural structures may prevent children from developing impulse control skills.

ADHD, Violence, and Delinquency

Other students who are considered at risk for committing delinquent and violent acts are children with attention deficit hyperactivity disorder (ADHD). In fact, the recent U.S. Surgeon General's report (2001) identified ADHD as a risk factor for violence in youths aged 6–11. According to Burrell and Warboys (2000) and Williams and Van Dorn (1999) four characteristics of ADHD—hyperactivity, concentration problems, restlessness, and risk-taking behaviors—have been found to be strong predictors of violent behavior (see table 3.2 for a list of ADHD characteristics). These characteristics, as well as poor social skills and certain beliefs and attitudes, such as seeing the need for retaliation, appear to favor the development of delinquent behavior. In addition, students with ADHD are more likely to display antisocial behavior, which is considered a risk factor for aggression later in adulthood and violent actions. Loeber (1996) points out that ADHD is also associated with early onset of delinquency and is correlated with persistent disruptive behavior.

Researchers have examined one or more of the ADHD characteristics and its relationship to violence or delinquent behavior. For example, concentration problems of boys ages 8 to 14 were significant predictors of self-reported violence and official arrests for violent offenses for males between the ages of 10 and 32 in a British study (Farrington 1989a). Klinteberg et al. (1993) examined restlessness (for example, difficulty sitting still, talkativeness) as measured by teacher reports and determined that restlessness is associated with later violence in adulthood. Several researchers (Hechtman and Weiss 1996; Loney, Kramer, and Milich 1983; Maguin et al. 1995; Mannuzza et al. 1989) have found that childhood hyperactivity is related to violence in adulthood. Others (Farrington 1989a, 1989b; Klinteberg et al. 1993; Maguin et al. 1995) have found that restlessness, poor concentration, impulsivity, and risk taking in childhood predict later violence. Hawkins et al. (1998) conducted a meta-analysis and found small positive correlations between childhood/adolescent hyperactivity, concentration problems, restlessness, and impulsivity.

One form of treatment for ADHD is Ritalin. O'Meara (2000) points out that many of the adolescent perpetrators in the high profiled school-yard shootings that occurred between 1996 and 1999 were taking psychotropic drugs, Ritalin, Prozac, and Luvox (see table 3.3). She states that these drugs have been known to cause psychotic episodes and violent behavior in some patients and may have played a part in the violent acts. In addition, she believes that although side effects have been recorded, the drugs continue to be prescribed at alarmingly high rates. "There are nearly 6 million children in the United States between the ages 6 and 18 taking mind-altering drugs prescribed for alleged illnesses that increasing numbers of mental health professional are questioning" (51). However, no research suggests there is a correlation between the recent cases of violent behavior in school-age children and the widespread use of psychotropic drugs such as Ritalin, Prozac, or Luvox.

SHOULD WE USE SPECIAL EDUCATION AS A SCHOOL VIOLENCE PREVENTION TECHNIQUE?

Some schools have responded to school violence by placing children in special education, while others are looking at the possibility of children

Table 3.3.   Ritalin, Prozac, and Luvox and School Shooters

Date	Shooter	Age	Medication
April 16	Shawn Cooper	15	Ritalin
April 20	Eric Harris	17	Luvox
May 20	T. J. Solomon	15	Ritalin
May 21	Kip Kinkel	15	Ritalin and Prozac

who have disabilities are at risk for committing violent acts. Although special education services are provided to students with special needs and these services help address individual student's needs such as aggressive behavior, special education should not be considered the solution for violence prevention, especially if the child is not eligible for special education services. Based on the Secret Service report (2002) we know that none of the targeted school shootings were committed by children with special needs.

CONCLUSION

Recent school-yard shootings have prompted researchers to focus on children with disabilities. "To what degree students with disabilities are responsible for disruption and violence is not clear, though at times public opinion places much of the blame squarely on special education students" (Smith 2001, 31). Although none of the school-yard shooters were identified as children with disabilities, children with disabilities may be at risk for committing violent acts, particularly children diagnosed with emotional disabilities and ADHD. Legislation protecting children with special needs has also been cited as a potential cause for school violence. However, this argument is unsubstantiated, especially since the U.S. General Accounting Office (2001) found that most principals believed that the law does not hinder their ability to keep and maintain a safe, productive learning environment. Legislators have amended IDEA giving the schools the ability to suspend violent students with disabilities for one year. However, even if a student with a disability is suspended, the school is mandated by IDEA to provide a free and appropriate education in the LRE. Some believe that the school should not be responsible for the education of students with disabilities once they are suspended; however, the law is clear that it is the school's responsibility to provide educational services. Furthermore, as noted in the General Accounting Office study, students with and without disabilities are disciplined in a similar manner and receive educational services equally. The next chapter provides a theoretical model of the ethic of care (Noddings 1984) and ecological model (Bronfenbrenner 1979), which suggests that not only is the school responsible for *all* children but that it requires everyone—parents, community, school personnel—to help prevent school violence.

REFERENCES

Amen, D. 1996. Brain SPECT findings and aggressiveness. *Annals of Clinical Psychiatry* 8(3): 129–37.

Barr, R. D., and W. H. Parrett. 2001. *Hope fulfilled for at-risk and violent youth: K–12 programs that work* (2d ed.). Boston: Allyn and Bacon.

Bender, W. N., T. H. Shubert, and P. J. McLaughlin. 2001. Invisible kids: Preventing school violence by identifying kids in trouble. *Intervention in School and Clinic* 37(2): 105.

Broder, P. K., N. Dunivant, E. C. Smith, and P. L. Suttin. 1981. Further observations on the link between learning disabilities and juvenile delinquency. *Journal of Educational Psychology* 73: 838–50.

Bronfenbrenner, U. (1979). *The ecology of human development: Experiments in nature and design*. Cambridge, Mass.: Harvard University Press.

Brower, M. C., and B. H. Price. 2001. Neuropsychiatry of frontal lobe dysfunction in violent and criminal behavior. *Journal of Neurology, Neurosurgery, & Psychiatry* 71: 720–26.

Burrell, S., and L. Warboys. 2000. Special education and the juvenile justice system. Office of Juvenile Justice Department, at www.ncjrs.org/html/ojjdp/2000_6_5/page1.html (accessed March 14, 2002).

Bush, G., Frazier, J. A., Rauch, S. L., Seidman, L. J., Whalen, P., Jenike, M. A., et al. 1999. Anterior cingulated cortex dysfunction in attention-deficit/hyperactivity disorder revealed by FMRI and the Counting Stroop. *Biological Psychiatry* 45(12): 1542–52.

Cahir, W. J. 2000. The Individuals with Disabilities Education Act contributes to violence in schools. In *School violence*, ed. J. Bryan Grapes, pp. 74–78. San Diego, Calif: Greenhaven.

Day, D. M., and A. C. Hunt. 1996. A multivariate assessment of a risk model for juvenile delinquency with an "under 12 offender" sample. *Journal of Emotional and Behavioral Disorders* 4: 66–72.

Farrington, D. P. 1989a. Early predictors of adolescent aggression and adult violence. *Violence and Victims* 4: 79–100.

Farrington, D. P. 1989b. Self-reporting and official offending from adolescence to adulthood. In *Cross-national research in self-reported crime and delinquency,* ed. M. Klein, pp. 339–423. Dordrecht, Netherlands: Kluwer.

Flannery, R. B. (1999). *Preventing youth violence: A guide for parents, teachers, and counselors*. New York: Continuum.

Hawkins, J. D., T. Herrenkohl, D P. Farrington, D. Brewer, R. F. Catalano, and T. W. Harachi. 1998. A review of predictors of youth violence. In *Serious & vi-*

olent juvenile offenders: Risk factors and successful intervention, ed. R. Loeber and D. P. Farrington, pp. 106–46. Thousand Oaks, Calif: Sage.

Hechtman, L., and G. Weiss. 1986. Controlled prospective fifteen-year follow-up of hyperactive adults: Nonmedical drug and alcohol use and anti-social behavior. *Canadian Journal of Psychiatry* 31: 557–67.

Indiana Department of Education. June 2000. Indiana State Board of Education. Special Education Rules. Title 511 Article 7. Rules 17–31. Indianapolis: Indiana Educational Resource Center.

Keiltz, I., and N. Dunivant. 1986. The relationship between learning disability and juvenile deliquency: Current state of knowledge. *Remedial and Special Education* 7(3): 18–26.

Klinteberg, B., T. Andersson, D. Magnusson, and H. Stattin. 1993. Hyperactive behavior in childhood as related to subsequent alcohol problems and violent offending: A longitudinal study of male subjects. *Personality and Individual Differences* 15: 381–88.

Loeber, R. 1996. Developmental continuity, change, and pathways in male juvenile problem behaviors and delinquency. In *Delinquency and crime: Current theories,* ed. J. D. Hawkins, pp. 1–27. New York: Cambridge University Press.

Loney, J., J. Kramer, and R. Milich. 1983. The hyperkinetic child grows up: Predictors of symptoms, delinquency, and achievement at follow-up: Birth and childhood cohorts. In *Handbook of longitudinal research* (vol. 1), ed. S. A. Mednick, M. Harway, and K. M. Finello. New York: Praeger.

Maguin, E., J. D. Hawkins, R. F. Catalano, K. Hill, R. Abbott, and T. Herrenkohl. 1995. November. *Risk factors measured at three ages for violence at age 17–18.* Paper presented at the American Society of Criminology, Boston.

Malmgren, K., R. D. Abbott, and J. D. Hawkins. 1999. LD and delinquency: Rethinking the link. *Journal of Learning Disabilities* 32: 194–200.

Mannuzza, S., R. G. Klein, P. H. Konig, and T. L. Giampino. 1989. Hyperactive boys almost grow up IV: Criminality and its relationship to psychiatric status. *Archives of General Psychiatry* 46: 1073–079.

Matthews, V. 2002, April. *Imaging studies in violence and aggression.* Paper presented at the 25th annual Arthur B. Richter Conference in Child Psychiatry: Recent Advances in Understanding and Treating Violence and Aggression in Children and Adolescents. Indiana University School of Medicine, Indianapolis.

Miller-Johnson, S., J. E. Coie, A. Maumary-Gremaud, J. Lockman, and R. Terry. 1999. Relationship between childhood peer rejection and aggression and adolescent delinquency severity and type among African American youth. *Journal of Emotional and Behavioral Disorders* 7: 137–46.

Murray, C. A. 1976. *The link between learning disabilities and juvenile delinquency: Current theory and knowledge.* Washington, D.C.: U.S. Government Printing Office.

Noddings, N. 1984. *Caring: A feminine approach to ethics and moral education.* Berkeley: University of California Press.

Perry, B. 1997. Incubated in terror: Neurodevelopment factors in the cycle of violence: In *Children in a violent society,* ed. J. Osofsky. New York Guilford Press.

Raine, A., J. R. Meloy, S. Bihrle, J. Stoddard, L. LaCasse, and M. S. Buchsbaum. 1998. Reduced prefrontal and increased subcortical brain functioning assessed using positron emission tomography in predatory and affective murders. *Behavior Science Law* 16: 319–32.

Rubia, K., S. Overmeyer, E. Taylor, M. Brammer, S. William, and A. Simmons, et al. 1999. Hypofrontality in attention deficit hyperactivity disorder during higher-order motor control: A study with functional MRI. *American Journal of Psychiatry* 156(6): 891–96.

Rudo, Z. H., V. Robbins, and D. Smith. 2002. Addressing home, school, and community violence for children with disabilities. In J. L. Paul, C. D. Lavely, A. Cranston-Gingras, and E. L. Taylor, ed. *Rethinking professional issues in special education.* Westport, Connecticut: Ablex Publishing.

Satterfield, J. H, C. M. Hoppe, and A. M. Schell. 1982. A prospective study of delinquency in 110 adolescent boys with attention deficit disorders and 88 normal boys. *American Journal of Psychiatry* 6: 795–98.

Shubert, T. H., S. Bressette, J. Deeken, and W. N. Bender. 1999. Analysis of random school shootings. In *Violence prevention and reduction in schools,* ed. W. N. Bender, G. Clinton, and R. L. Bender. Austin, Texas: PRO-ED.

Smith, C. R. 2000. Behavioral and discipline provisions of IDEA '97: Implicit competencies yet to be confirmed. *Exceptional Children* 66(3): 403–12.

SRI International. 1993. National Longitudinal Transition Study, U.S. Department of Special Education, at www.sri.com/policy/cehs/publications/dispub/nlts/nltssum.html (accessed March 11, 2002).

Tobin, T. J., and G. M. Sugai. 1999. Using sixth grade school records to predict school violence, chronic discipline problems, and high school outcomes. *Journal of Emotional and Behavioral Disorders* 7: 40–53.

Trump, K. S. 1999. *Stopping school violence: An essential guide.* Gaithersburg, Md.: Aspen.

U.S. Department of Education. 1998. *The twentieth annual report to Congress on the implementation of Individuals with Disabilities Education Act.* Washington, D.C.: U.S. Government Printing Office.

U.S. General Accounting Office. 2001. Student discipline, Individuals with Disabilities Education Act, A report to the Committee on Appropriations, U.S. Senate and House of Representatives, Washington, D.C. available www.gao.gov/new.items/d01210.pdf.

U.S. Secret Service and U.S. Department of Education. 2002. The final report and findings of the safe school initiative: Implications for the prevention of school attacks in the United States, at www.secretservice.gov/ntac/ntac_ssi_report.pdf (accessed February 22, 2002).

U.S. Surgeon General. 2001. *Youth violence: A report of the surgeon general.* Washington D.C.: U.S. Surgeon General's Office, at surgeongeneral.gov.library/youthviolence/toc.html (accessed February 22, 2002).

Volkow, N. D., L. R. Tancredi, C. Grant, and H. Gillespie, et al. 1995. Brain glucose metabolism in violent psychiatric patients: A preliminary study. *Psychiatry Research: Neuroimaging* 61(4): 243–53.

Walker, H. M., and R. Sylvester. 1994. Where is school along the path to prison? *The Frontline* 1: 3–6.

Weinberger, D. 2002. The immaturity of the adolescent brain can lead to school shootings. In *School shooting,* ed. Laura Egendorf. San Diego, Calif.: Greenhaven.

Williams, J. H., and R. A. Van Dorn. 1999. Delinquency, gangs, and youth violence. In *Youth violence: Current research and recent practice innovations,* ed. J. M. Jenson and M. O. Howard. Washington, D.C.: NASW Press.

Chapter Four

Theoretical Underpinnings: The Ecological Perspective and an Ethic of Care

Patricia A. Parrish

In the late 1970s, Uri Bronfenbrenner described his theory of human development. This theory is based on a child's interaction within his environments. Beginning in the 1980s, Nel Noddings described a school environment in which teachers and students engage in caring relationships. These two theories can be combined to provide insights into reducing school violence.

This chapter explains the ecology of human development and an ethic of care. Once the theoretical underpinnings have been laid, they will be connected as a prelude to making applications to the issue of school violence.

THE ECOLOGY OF HUMAN DEVELOPMENT

Bronfenbrenner (1979) describes a theory of human development that includes the child's ecological context as crucial to development. Within this theory, Bronfenbrenner describes several systems in which a child participates, either directly or indirectly. These systems directly influence the development of the child and of others who also interact within the systems. These concentric systems, or levels, identified by Bronfenbrenner include the microsystem, mesosystem, exosystem, and macrosystem.

The *microsystem,* the most intimate of the systems, is defined as a "pattern of activities, roles, and interpersonal relations experienced by the developing person in a given face-to-face setting with particular physical and material features, and containing other persons with distinctive characteristics of

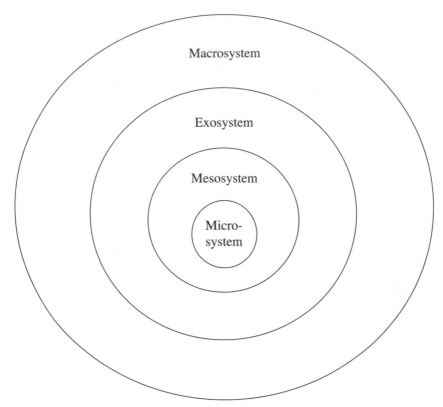

Figure 4.1. Bronfenbrenner's (1979) Ecology of Human Development

temperament, personality, and systems of belief" (Bronfenbrenner 1992, 227). The microsystem incorporates the physical environment and the people in the environment with whom the child interacts (Sontag 1996). Examples of microsystems include the family and the classroom. Within the classroom, we can look at the teacher–child relationship and the peer–child relationships. Additionally, the microsystem incorporates the perceptions of those involved. This has important implications for the analysis of the classroom environment. It is not enough for an observer to record what she sees in the quality of the interactions between teacher and students, it is also important to understand how the teacher and the students each interpret the quality of interaction. This phenomenological approach to understanding development forces us to move beyond the empirical to the interactional as we try and understand violence in schools.

The next level in which a child develops is the mesosystem. The *mesosystem* is defined as "the interrelations among two or more settings in which the developing person becomes an active participant" (Bronfenbrenner and Hamilton 1978, 3). In other words, the mesosystem contains two or more microsystems. For a typical youth, these might be the interconnections between home, school, and neighborhood. For a school to be effective, there must be connections between the microsystems of the classroom and the other microsystems in which students interact.

The exosystem is the third level of the concentric system. The *exosystem* "is an extension of the mesosystem involving settings that do not themselves contain the developing person as an active participant, but in which events occur that affect, and occasionally are affected by that person" (Bronfenbrenner and Hamilton 1978, 4). Examples of the exosystem may include the parents' place of work, the state legislature that enacts a new curriculum, the teachers' workroom, and a sibling's school. The school-age child is often very aware of the exosystem acting upon him, instead of him acting upon the system. Such a sense can cause some children to feel disempowered, especially if their microsystems do not cause them to feel valued as individuals.

The fourth level of the hierarchy is the *macrosystem*, which

> consists of the overarching pattern of micro-, meso-, and exosystems characteristic of a given culture, subculture, or other broader social context, with particular reference to the developmentally instigative belief systems, resources, hazards, life styles, opportunity structures, life course options, and patterns of social interchange that are embedded in each of these systems. The macrosystem may be thought of as a societal blueprint for a particular culture, subculture, or other broader social context. (Bronfenbrenner 1992, 228)

The macrosystem encompasses the core belief system within the society at large. This system will have a direct effect on all the lower-level systems described by Bronfenbrenner. Because of society's expectations for a school's function, classrooms across the society are very similar. The macrosystem (societal belief) directly affects the child's microsystem (the classroom) and therefore the child's development and perception of the world.

Bronfenbrenner's model has important implications for schools. Schools need to be aware of the impact policies have on classroom environments

and on the development of the children who interact within these classrooms. Literature on the ethic of care can also be viewed through the lens
of the ecological perspective. To establish a conversation on the ecological
perspective and creating caring classrooms, the ethic of care needs to be
addressed.

THE ETHIC OF CARE

Bronfenbrenner's ecological theory can help us to understand the role of
caring in the classroom. Rogers and Webb (1991) describe teaching as a
moral activity in which teachers need to examine the ethical implications
of their actions. This implies that teachers need to go beyond actions to
look at the effect of these actions on relationships and across Bronfenbrenner's systems. Because an ethic of care emphasizes relationships and
responsibilities, rather than rules and rights, it can be viewed as a moral
activity (Rogers and Webb 1991). Glasser (1975) identifies two basic
needs: (a) the need to love and be loved, and (b) the need to feel worthwhile. These two needs are intricately related to care in that genuine caring meets the basic need for security and attachment (or loving and being
loved) and, beyond that, connects people to a "self-perpetuating cycle of
'natural' and ethical caring" (Rogers and Webb 1991). This cycle promotes self-worth in those who participate in it, thus fulfilling Glasser's
second basic need, the need to feel worthwhile. This feeling of self-worth
can also help a child overcome the feeling of disempowerment that occurs
when the mesosystem acts upon him.

Though caring has been relatively ignored as part of the teaching equa-
tion for children with problems, Morse (1994) identifies it as "the experience desperately needed, especially by troubled children and those at risk"
(132). One possible reason to view care as essential to the development,
education, and healing of troubled students, and to the optimal development of all students, might be that care moves a person from the idea of
merely not hurting another to the possibility of responding actively to self
and others in order to sustain a connection (Gilligan 1982). This sustained
connection becomes the basis of a caring relationship, one that can help
troubled youth heal themselves with the guidance and support of a dedicated teacher. Before establishing such a connection, troubled youth may

have difficulty meeting the initial injunction of not hurting others, let alone moving to the idea of sustaining relationships. It may not be reasonable to expect teachers and schools to heal the deepest wounds of children who are most damaged from emotional trauma, but these children can still be taught what it means to care and to be cared for (Noddings 1991; Morse 1994). It is for these children who may have never experienced caring relationships that schools need to make caring a priority (Noddings 1991). Nevertheless, Jensen and Jensen (1998) found that "the school environment is the one which emphasizes caring the least" (834) when compared with family, media, peer, and religious environments. This has strong implications for a child's interactions within the microsystem of the classroom.

Caring can be viewed from different perspectives, most notably as virtue or ethic. Both of these views can be supported in philosophic writings, but the more commonly accepted today seems to be that caring is an ethic involving relationship (Gilligan 1982; Noddings 1984, 1992; Ruddick 1989). Several authors credit the shift from caring as a virtue to caring as a relational ethic to the feminist movement and feminist standpoint theory (Noddings 1984; Ruddick 1989). Before the birth of feminism, masculine societies associated caring with weakness because it was a woman's role to care for the family and women were seen as the weaker gender. For men to find caring acceptable, or not weak, abstract views of "truth" and "caring" emerged. These abstract views were detached from feelings, self, and body (Ruddick 1989). Therefore, caring was viewed as a virtue devoid of feeling and thus became acceptable to masculine leaders. The leaders of the world were expected to make decisions based on what was truthful and right, not what felt good or helped others to feel good. From this perspective, it is easy to view caring for another person as helping that person to grow and self-actualize (Mayeroff 1971)—the person providing care needs to give what that person thinks is "best" for the other person, whether or not the other person actually recognizes or agrees that this is caring. This perspective seems to ignore the perception of the one being cared for, yet perception has been identified as an essential component of the microsystem.

Noddings (1984) uses the term *aesthetical caring* to describe what has been called the virtue of care. She uses this term to talk about caring for things and ideas, a qualitatively different type of care than that in which two human beings engage. Aesthetical caring is unidirectional and does not need to be received by the cared-for (the object) to be deemed caring. The difference between aesthetical caring and traditional masculine, or unidirectional, caring is that aesthetical caring can only be visited upon inanimate objects (excluding even plants and animals) while masculine care is applied to all things animate or inanimate. However, it is important to note that not only males engage in masculine caring or that only females engage in relational caring but rather that these types of care have traditionally been credited as masculine or feminine.

While the perspective shown here highlights caring as relational, the reader is still left asking what caring *is*. Providing a definition seems to be very personal, and each theorist seems to have his or her own view. Yet one thing is certain: we all know *it* when we see *it* (Rogers and Webb 1991). *The American College Dictionary* defines *care* as "worry, anxiety . . . serious attention . . . protection . . . an object of concern . . . to be concerned . . . (and) to have an inclination, liking, fondness, or affection" (181–82). It is important to note that this definition does not include any mention of a relationship, and only in the later meanings does it reflect the idea of affection or inclination. Surely, schools need to base a curriculum of care on more than a concern or worry; this is where a feminine perspective comes in.

The basis for feminine perspective can be found in the philosophical works of Wittgenstein, Habermas, and Winch, who support the idea that thought grows out of and is shaped by the activities in which one engages. Since women traditionally engage in caring, this can be the beginning of thought and should not be separated from all other endeavors, as it would devalue its place (Ruddick 1989). This position supports care and caring as the epistemological and political foundation of feminist standpoint theory.

Moving from this beginning, Noddings (1984) notes that when caring is directed toward living things, it is crucial to consider their ways of life, natures, desires, and needs. Thus caring is moving away from a unidirectional virtue and into a relational act. If one must consider the ways and beliefs of the other during the provision of care, one must begin to allow feelings to enter into the relationship. Ruddick (1989) supports this view when she claims that "a death that is cared for is actively nonviolent" (215). If the difference between a violent and nonviolent death is care, then care must take into account the feelings of the one who is dying for it is the person, not the survivors, for whom death would be deemed violent. Therefore, it can be extrapolated that care, in its natural form, can further be defined to encompass the most intimate situations of human existence (Noddings 1984). By definition, the intimate environments in which children engage are those in the microsystem.

Watson (1988) developed a value system of human care. This system grew out of the field of nursing, but is equally appropriate in any profession that centers on valuing human beings and their growth or development. Watson's system values and deeply respects the mysteries and wonders of life; acknowledges the spiritual dimension of life, growth, and change; requires high reverence and regard for humans and human life; and respects values related to autonomy (nonpaternalistic) and freedom of choice. If this defines *care,* is it any wonder that today's schools, which are dedicated to conformity and assessment like their predecessors, fail to provide care to and with their students?

Caring can be constructed on many different levels which can be viewed as concentric circles (Noddings 1984). The innermost of these circles includes caring for those we love. This type of caring is seldom felt as a requirement or duty but rather it is the type of caring in which we want to engage. It comes to us naturally, like the cared-for death described earlier.

The next circle includes caring for those for whom we have personal regard. This would again be natural; it includes caring for friends and neighbors. The next circle involves caring for those to whom we feel chains of caring. This is the level that includes people to whom we have become "chained" when they entered our lives, often unbidden. This category of caring includes the students who enter our classrooms each fall with the hopes and expectations of youth. We may not have any reason outside of the "chain" to engage in caring with these people, but because of the "chain" we are obligated to care for them now. The last of the concentric circles of caring encompasses caring for strangers. This would include sending donations to help those who are starving overseas or participating in demonstrations directed at changing policies that oppress citizens of foreign countries. While we are obligated to engage in caring relationships with those in the inner circles because of their presence in our lives, we are under no such obligations to care for those in the outermost circle—yet most humane adults are moved to care for a stranger at some point in their lives. This type of caring can be very intense when it occurs and can have lasting effects on the caring we engage in with those in our inner circles.

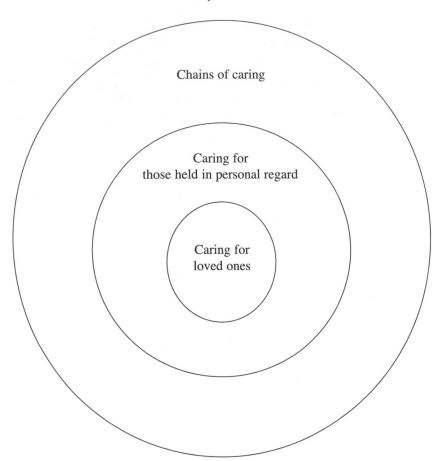

Figure 4.2.   Noddings's (1984) Concentric Circles of Caring

Watson has taken the concept of care as a relationship into the realm of action. She tells us that "the essence of the value of human care and caring may be futile unless it contributes to a philosophy of action" (Watson 1988, 32). This would indicate that beyond entering into a relationship of care, this relationship needs to include an act of caring. The activities involved in caring are numerous and can be exhibited through the maintenance of shelter, sustenance of a circle of connections, attainment and production of food, attention to the vulnerable, or teaching of the previously untaught (Ruddick 1989). This type of care can be practiced only interpersonally (Watson 1988), thus inextricably weaving a web of caring relationships and actions—one cannot effectively occur in the absence of the other.

Noddings (1984, 1992) explains the concept of active caring as a relationship between the "one-caring" and the "cared-for." Such a relationship must be reciprocal. For caring to be sustained, the "one-caring" must receive some sort of reward from the one "cared-for." In the case of an infant, the "cared-for" is able to return smiles, cuddles, and love to the "one-caring." Noddings goes on to distinguish this type of caring from aesthetic caring based on the reciprocity of the relationship. The "one-caring" neither expects nor receives a reward when providing care to an inanimate object. One can, however, be rewarded by the growth of a plant or the wagging tail of a dog, thus moving care for plants and animals into the area of active caring, important to classrooms in which students engage in growing plants or caring for pets. As the "cared-for" grows in ability to reinforce caring, the expectations of such reinforcement can and do change. A maturing child is expected to at times take on the role of "one-caring" rather than being solely the "cared-for." Typically, this role shift begins with the care of a plant or an animal; sometimes it can begin with the care of a younger sibling.

Eventually, the maturing child is able to engage in more complex relationships, where at times she will fulfill the role of "one-caring" and at times the role of "cared-for" with the same individual. In school, this relationship can take place between students and/or between a student and a teacher. The ability to move between these two roles with the same partner in care can be seen as a hallmark of growth and development, yet may be one of the greatest challenges faced by students with emotional and behavioral disorders.

Smith and Emigh (1999) identify a four-part model of caring based on the feminine perspective, which they have applied to education. The model includes the dynamics of care, caring behaviors, construction of a caring environment, and modeling and facilitating caring in others.

The dynamics of care include the relationships that occur between teachers and students (Smith and Emigh 1999). Teachers who display this dynamic have a positive regard for students, are committed, are open to receiving their students' perspectives, respond to these perspectives, and remain present to their students (Beck 1992; Noddings 1984; Smith and Emigh 1999). Behaviors that would be congruent with this dynamic include engaging students in communication and then responding to their statements, smiling at students, and being available to students who seek help (Beck 1992).

The second aspect of the model is caring behaviors. These include behaviors that address academic, social, and affective areas (Smith and Emigh 1999). Such behaviors might include providing appropriate instruction paced to meet student needs; sharing who they are with students; using positive, open body language; and communicating a passion for learning and teaching (Agne 1992; Smith 1995).

The construction of a caring environment is the third part of the model. This includes both the physical and the emotional space within the classroom. Behaviors associated with this include consistently rewarding appropriate behavior, using communication skills to reduce student anxiety, adherence to routines and rituals, and celebration and affirmation of individual differences (Bulach, Brown, and Potter 1996; Byrd et al. 1996; Noblit 1993).

The last part of this model is facilitating the development of caring. These are the processes in the classroom through which the teacher helps students learn how to care for others. Behaviors related to this include modeling caring thoughts and behaviors, advocating for students with others (including supervising teachers and administrators), and respecting individuals (Agne 1992; Smith and Emigh 1999).

The four-part model of caring identified here has found limited support in research involving the students' perspective of care (Parrish 2001). Parrish found that students perceived teacher caring as falling into three of the four categories identified by Smith and Emigh (1999). These included (a) the dynamics of care, (b) caring behaviors, and (c) facilitating the development of care. The dynamics of care include a teacher's positive regard for students, openness to student perspective, being present to students, and celebrating and affirming individual differences. Caring behaviors include a teacher's ability to address academic, social, affective, and physical needs of the students. Facilitating the development of care includes modeling caring for and about oneself, modeling caring behaviors, respecting individuals, and advocating for students with others. These aspects of caring are interwoven, meaning that students cannot completely separate one from the other in their memories of caring teachers. These student perceptions of caring are critical when looking at Bronfenbrenner's description of the microsystem and its application to schools. Because the participants perceptions of the personal relationship largely impact their development, we cannot fully discuss the effect of caring on the microsystem without addressing the student's perspective of caring.

AN ETHIC OF CARE AND THE ECOLOGICAL PERSPECTIVE

Connecting an ethic of care with the ecological perspective is easy if the starting point is the concentric circles described within each (Bronfenbrenner 1979; Noddings 1984). Both theories place intimate relationships at their core and move out to examine less personal relationships, while recognizing the influence of these on the intimate levels.

Noddings (1984) describes caring for loved ones as the most central type of caring. It can easily be extrapolated that those we love would be part of our microsystem, the level of ecological theory dealing with personal relationships. Interestingly, Bronfenbrenner places the classroom environment within the microsystem, yet Noddings places the teacher–student relationship in one of her outer circles, chains of caring. This mismatch could explain why students find the classroom to be one of the places that are least caring (Jensen and Jensen 1998). It would seem that for the classroom to truly become a place of optimal development for the child, as indicated by its place in Bronfenbrenner's hierarchy, there is a need for teachers and students to move their relationship to Noddings's inner circle of caring. Since most adults are able to remember a teacher they believe cared about them, and maybe even one whom they loved and feel loved them, it seems that some classroom relationships do move to Noddings's inner circle. It is not realistic, however, to assume that every teacher and every student will be able to move into a relationship of love. Perhaps a more likely scenario is one in which teacher and student can move into Noddings's middle circle, personal regard.

The move from chained caring to personal regard might be facilitated if teachers help build relationships with their students by attending to the student perception of caring as outlined in Parrish (2001). Through this approach, the teacher can ensure personal sharing with students in a way that is likely to be perceived as caring by the students. Such teachers place self-development at the center of their teaching persona. Moustakas (1966) suggests three ways to contribute to this development: (a) confirming the child as worth; (b) being authentically present, open, and honest in student interaction; and (c) making resources available. If teachers can engage their students in such a manner, they are likely to move into a relationship of personal regard. Such a relationship should support the development of reciprocal caring and thereby begin the healing process for troubled youth, as suggested by Noddings (1991) and Morse (1994).

Palmer (1998) also sheds light on ways the student–teacher relationship can move from chained caring to one of the inner circles of caring, personal regard, or caring for loved ones. Palmer believes an effective teacher is able to establish a rapport that leads to friendship. This does not happen by accident; it happens because teachers know themselves and see "themselves" as a crucial component of good teaching. They are able to recognize that feelings influence the exchange between teacher and student, as well as the context in which these exchanges occur. Teachers who are able to do this seem to be incorporating context and perception into the creation of the microsystem of the classroom. They are accepting their students as individuals and allowing the student perspective to become a part of the context, equally as important as the teacher perspective.

CONCLUSION

This chapter has outlined the basic tenets of Bronfenbrenner's ecology of human development theory. This theory of human development posits that a child's development is effected by the environments in which he or she lives. This hierarchical system can be viewed as the microsystem, mesosystem, exosystem, and macrosystem. Interactions within and across these levels will have direct effect on a child's development.

The ethic of care is based on relational caring between two living beings. It is based on the concept that people will respond to and build caring relationships with others who respond to their hopes, desires, and needs. This relationship can become the basis of personal growth for both of the participants. According to Noddings (1984), the relationship between a student and a teacher is one of the least intensive levels of caring. Yet, this chapter has begun to look at ways the intensity of caring can be increased in an attempt to move toward the core of caring, hoping to achieve congruence with Bronfenbrenner who has placed the student–teacher relationship at the core of the ecological perspective.

REFERENCES

Agne, K. J. 1992. Caring: The expert teacher's edge. *Educational Horizons* 70(3): 120–24.

Beck, L. G. 1992. Meeting the challenge of the future: The place of a caring ethic in educational administration. *American Journal of Education* 100(4): 454–96.

Bronfenbrenner, U. 1979. *The ecology of human development: Experiments in nature and design*. Cambridge, Mass.: Harvard University Press.

Bronfenbrenner, U. 1992. Ecological systems theory. In *Annals of child development. Six theories of child development: Revised formulations and current issues,* ed. R. Vasta, pp. 287–309. Heidelberg: Springer-Verlag.

Bronfenbrenner, U., and S. F. Hamilton. 1978. *School effectiveness in ecological perspective*. Prepared for the Conference on School Organization and Effects sponsored by the National Institute of Education, San Diego (ERIC Document Reproduction Service ED 182 371).

Bulach, C., C. Brown, and L. Potter. 1996. *Behaviors that create a caring learning community*. Paper presented at the Annual Meeting of the Southern Regional Council on Education Administration, Savannah, Ga. (ERIC Document Reproduction Services ED 401 641).

Byrd, J., M. Lundeberg, S. Hoffland, E. Couillard, and M. Lee. 1996. Caring, cognition, and cultural pluralism: Case studies of urban teachers. *Urban Education* 31(4): 432–52.

Gilligan, C. 1982. *In a different voice: Psychological theory and women's development.* Cambridge, Mass.: Harvard University Press.

Glasser, W. 1975. *Reality therapy: A new approach to psychiatry.* New York: Harper & Row.

Jensen, L. C., and L. N. Jensen. 1998. Adolescents' perceptions of caring in family, media, school, peer, and religious environments. *Psychological Reports* 82: 832–34.

Mayeroff, M. 1971. *On Caring.* New York: Harper & Row.

Morse, W. C. 1994. The role of caring in teaching children with behavior problems. *Contemporary Education* 65(3): 132–36.

Moustakas, C. 1966. *The authentic teacher: Sensitivity and awareness in the classroom.* Cambridge, Mass.: Howard A. Doyle.

Noblit, G. W. 1993. Power and caring. *American Educational Research Journal* 30(1): 23–38.

Noddings, N. 1984. *Caring: A feminine approach to ethics and moral education.* Berkeley: University of California Press.

Noddings, N. 1991. Stories in dialogue: Caring and interpersonal reasoning. In *Stories lives tell: Narrative and dialogue in education,* ed. C. Witherell and N. Noddings, pp. 157–70. New York: Teachers College Press.

Noddings, N. 1992. *The challenge to care in schools: An alternate approach to education.* New York: Teachers College Press.

Palmer, P. J. 1998. *The courage to teach: Exploring the inner landscape of a teacher's life.* New York: Jossey-Bass.

Parrish, P. A. 2001. *Developing an understanding of caring: Preservice and in-service teachers' memories of caring in the classroom.* Unpublished doctoral dissertation, University of South Florida.

Rogers, D., and J. Webb. 1991. The ethic of caring in teacher education. *Journal of Teacher Education* 42(3): 173–81.

Ruddick, S. 1989. *Maternal thinking.* Boston: Beacon Press.

Smith, B. 1995. That's no techno-fix. *Phi Delta Kappan* 76(9): 659.

Smith, R. L., and L. Emigh. 1999. A model for defining the construct of caring in teacher education. Unpublished manuscript, University of South Florida, Sarasota.

Sontag, J. C. 1996. Toward a comprehensive theoretical framework for disability research: Bronfenbrenner revisited. *The Journal of Special Education* 30(3): 319–44.

Watson, J. 1988. *Nursing: Human science and human care a theory of nursing.* New York: National League for Nursing.

Chapter Five

Prevention of School Violence

Denise Smith and Patricia A. Parrish

The American public has been shocked and dismayed by the lethality and seriousness of school-yard shootings over the past several years. Many still remember the massacre at Columbine High School on April 20, 1999, when Eric Harris and Dylan Klebold shot and killed twelve students and one teacher; wounded twenty-three other students; and then committed suicide. Despite this rash of targeted school-yard shootings, research suggests that school violence is declining. According to the National School Safety Center (2000), the total number of violent death incidents has declined from a high of fifty-five during the 1992–1993 school year to thirty-four during the 1998–1999 school year. Less than 1 percent of 1,354 children nationwide who were murdered during the 1998–1999 school year were school associated (National School Safety Center 2000). Research findings also suggest that fewer children are bringing guns to school. During the 1990s, there was a steady decline from 17 percent to 12 percent of students in grades 9 through 12 who reported carrying a weapon to school (U.S. Department of Education 2000). However, the Hamilton Fish Institute (2000) found that there are 100 times more guns in the hands of children attending American schools than principals have been reporting to Congress. Regardless of these conflicting statistics, if only one child brings a gun to school, the lives of all children are threatened.

Schools are currently faced with the dilemma of dealing with the school-yard shootings, especially since teachers and students are expressing concern about the safety of their school. Too often teachers and students feel unsafe in the school environment and are experiencing violence directly. Besides creating fear in everyone, school violence is diverting energy and resources from instruction (Ascher 1994). Not surprisingly, the seventh National Education Goal of Goals 2000 calls for "safe, disciplining, and drug free schools that offer an environment conducive to learning" (Ascher 1994, 1).

Forty-four percent of students say they feel "a lot" of responsibility for keeping their school safe (Metropolitan Life 2000). In fact, many students are being asked to help stop the shootings before they occur. According to a post-Columbine study conducted by the U.S. Secret Service (2002), in more than 75 percent of school violence incidents, the school-yard shooters gave either spoken or written warning signs. Students are being urged to come forward with information about potential school shootings. Some students are responding. For example, Victoria Sudd, 17, from Twenty-nine Palms, California, told her mom that she overheard two boys making comments on the bus about killing kids. Sudd's parents contacted the police, who searched the boys' homes and found a rifle and a list of sixteen students whom the boys allegedly were going to shoot.

Given the complexity of the school-yard shootings, one would expect school interventions to be multifaceted. Unfortunately, most school violence interventions focus on only one or two variables at one ecological level (Jenson and Howard 1999). For example, some schools have resorted to installing warning devices such as metal detectors for detecting weapons on children, increasing police protection, searching students and lockers, and requiring students and staff to wear identification cards. However, there is little evidence to support these prevention techniques, which focus on only the student (Hyman and Snook 2000; Skiba and Peterson 2000).

Other schools have resorted to drastic interventions such as referral to special education, school transfer, suspension, and expulsion. According to the National School Safety Center (2000), during the 1998–1999 academic school year, various states reported that they had expelled an estimated 3,523 students for bringing a firearm to school. Forty-four percent of students expelled for firearms were referred to an alternative school. Still other schools are resorting to zero-tolerance policies and requiring teachers to report any sign of violence, including references made by students either spoken or written in journals or essays. This precaution takes into consideration the fact that most of the school-yard shooters had made numerous threats or wrote about the violent acts they intended to do.

As mentioned previously, school intervention programs that focus on only one variable at one ecological level such as the zero-tolerance policy, suspension, or expulsion tend not to be effective in reducing levels of school violence (Barr and Parrett 2001). Instead, school interventions need to address all variables at all ecological levels. Drawing on Bronfenbrenner's (1979) ecological levels and adapting an ethos of care espoused by Noddings (1984), schools could accomplish this.

THE NEED FOR THE ETHIC OF CARE AS A SCHOOL INTERVENTION

"Violent youth feel like they are outsiders, that no one cares for them, that no one cares about them" (Barr and Parrett 2001).

Teachers have an enormous impact on children, either negative or positive. Research has documented how important it is for students to have a positive connection with teachers. In fact, the U.S. Secret Service (2002) reported that the best strategy for reducing youth risk factors and crime was having the child/youth establish positive caring connections to an adult. Resnick et al. (1997) found that positive relationships with teachers have been found to be significant in protecting teenagers from engaging in negative behavior.

Not only do teachers have an impact on children, but also the school environment. A recent article in *USA Today* (Harrington-Lueker 2001) laments the idea of large middle schools that isolate and alienate our teenagers. Kantrowitz and Wingert (1999) echo the same concern and state, "In survey after survey, many kids—even those on honor roll—say they feel increasingly alone and alienated, unable to connect to their parents, teachers, and sometimes even classmates" (36). Many agree that middle schools and high schools are far too big (National Association of Secondary Principals 1996). In fact, the U.S. Department of Education (1998) has recommended creating smaller schools for high-risk students.

In addition to teachers and the school environment, parents also play a pivotal role in decreasing violent acts of behavior. However, several parents of school-age children work, resulting in more children coming home from school to an empty house. Not surprisingly, the Office of Juvenile Justice and Delinquency Prevention (1999) found that violent acts of crime committed by children occur immediately after school hours. The investigators also found that this is the time of day when children are more likely to become victims of crimes. These statistics accentuate the need for adapting an ethos of care.

CARE AND EDUCATION

As mentioned previously, the U.S. Secret Service (2002) believes that when children/youth establish a caring, connected relationship with an adult they are less likely to participate in school violence. To this end, the following section describes Noddings's ethic of care and, based on her theory, the empirical evidence that supports students having caring connections with an adult. Several educators have proposed a caring-focused approach to education (Eisner 1997; Noblit 1993; Noddings 1984, 1992). Within such an approach, attention to student needs and desires becomes a central factor (Noddings 1992).

After the formation of caring relationships with teachers over time, students are helped to focus their learning on areas of interest while being encouraged to take risks and attempt difficult tasks by and with a connected teacher (Noddings 1992). Student achievement would vary more than in current systems as students develop based on different talents and intelligences. Such an approach to schooling would encourage students to pursue their interests and would create the need for a broadened curriculum, rather than a narrow one that forces "all students [to run] down the same track, measured by the same tests, and whose performance is reported out to the third or fourth decimal place" (Eisner 1997, 271).

Such an approach to education would help all students, especially those with emotional and behavioral differences, to overcome attachment difficulties (Morse 1994), a first step to successful healing. Once this begins to happen, students will be able to focus on the learning and risk taking associated with learning by and with a connected teacher (Noddings 1992). Yet very little research focuses on the idea of a caring curriculum and its necessary teacher–student relationships. The study of caring and caring behaviors may help educators begin to value caring explicitly, making it an equal priority with the achievement-oriented aspects of teaching and learning (Smith and Emigh 1999).

CARING AND GOOD TEACHING

Effective school research supports the need for adapting an ethic of care in schools. When we, as teachers, confirm caring acts, we help our students become aware of themselves as ethical and intellectual beings who are capable of either nurturing—or destroying—an ethic of caring (Rogers and Webb 1991).

When guided by an ethic of care, teachers make decisions about their students based on the students' needs and expected responses (Noddings 1991). Such decisions can occur only when teachers and students enter into dialogue over time, thus providing support for the idea of teachers and students staying together for several years (Noddings 1991). In fact, the U.S. Surgeon General (2001) reported continuous progress (also known as *looping*) as an effective technique for preventing school violence. Such long-term relationships give students and teachers time to develop caring and to gain necessary skills in dialogue, and for students to become caregivers as modeled by the teacher (Noddings 1991).

Daly (1985) describes one educational approach used in British schools for students with emotional and behavioral disorders. This approach is premised on the idea that a compassionate attitude toward students would improve outcomes more than the traditional, medical model approaches. Teachers involved in this study perceived better classroom relationships among students, increased problem-solving skills in students, decreased disruptions in the classroom, and increased task completion among students. In other words, these students increased the skills needed for improved performance on accountability tests.

Linkous (1989) studied two classrooms looking at relationships between teachers and their students. He found that teachers talked about caring with their students and used verbal and nonverbal interactions to communicate their message. Such an approach, dialogue linked with modeling, also receives theoretical support (Noddings 1995).

Another study looked at the teacher–student relationship through in-depth case study. Noblit (1993) completed a yearlong ethnography of an elementary school classroom where he looked at issues of caring and power. He found that Pam, the teacher, used the power she had to focus on collectivity rather than competition. Additionally, Pam's power focused on building her students and their confidence. She used routines to create a comfortable environment in which her students would thrive. Noblit concluded that caring is about the ethical use of power by the teacher, not about an equal sharing of power between teacher and students. Entering into this study, Noblit expected to learn that power and caring were separate entities and he states that he learned as much from Pam in that year as did any of her "other" students.

Collinson, Killeavy, and Stephenson (1999) conducted a study that supported Noblit's (1993) findings that power and caring are related. This study focused on exemplary teachers in England, Ireland, and the United States. The teachers in this study substituted respect for authority and power and also saw an ethic of care as the basis for learning.

In a study of effective teachers reputed as caring, Lambert (1995) identified several characteristics of teachers who were effective and caring. One of the most striking beliefs of these teachers is the central place of caring in creating effective classrooms. Other identified characteristics include proficiency with technical aspects of teaching, flexibility, alertness or with-it-ness, reflectivity, persistence, humility, and tolerance. The teachers in this study taught in both special and general education settings.

After completing an ethnographic case study of urban elementary school teachers looking for characteristics of "community," Kratzer (1996) found that caring was an important element of community. Teachers in this school promoted and valued diversity, created formal structures to increase empowerment and ownership, legitimated the affective aspect of schooling, and expected reciprocal relationships with students and their parents.

STUDENT PERSPECTIVE ON CARING

"A recurring theme in students' comments is the tremendous value they place on having teachers who care" (Phelan, Davidson, and Cao 1992, 698). These researchers conducted a study of fifty-four high school students during a two-year period. They found that student perceptions of caring are remarkably similar to teacher perceptions. Students indicated that they responded better to teachers who took a genuine interest in their well-being, who actively engaged them in learning, who were patient, and who willingly engaged in conversation. These attributes were especially important to low-achieving students.

Siddle-Walker (1993) completed a historical ethnography of a good school that had served African American students during segregation. This study looked at the perceptions of administration, faculty, parents, and students. In this school, caring was a daily practice with teachers asking about student problems and establishing high expectations for student performance. She found that former students of the Caswell County Training School spoke of "father-like" and "mother-like" former teachers. Siddle-Walker (1993) concluded that interpersonal caring was at the base of academic success in the school. Students did not want to let their teachers down because of the caring relationships that allowed familylike interaction and provided encouragement and support.

Through the use of focus groups, participant observation, in-depth interview, and document review, Van Galen (1996) found that students in a Catholic high school reputed as very caring identified program strengths in the areas of personal interaction, use of humor, and personal involvement of the faculty. The personal interaction included both academic help and personal issues/counseling. While most instruction was delivered through whole-group lecture, one-on-one help was provided as needed.

The following section describes school violence prevention/intervention strategies identified by the U.S. Surgeon General (2001) that can be used to reduce violence and serious delinquency and risk factors of violence. The Surgeon General systematically examined the literature on youth prevention/intervention strategies and classified them as either effective or ineffective. The prevention/intervention strategies identified as effective were further broken down into model programs and promising programs. Therefore, the prevention/intervention best practices presented are described as such (see table 5.1).

Developing a conceptual model is important to guide teachers and teacher educators for preventing violence. Thus Noddings's and Bronfenbrenner's theories undergird the strategies presented. Bronfenbrenner's model provides a framework for analyzing the types of interactions necessitated to decrease school violence. This provides a way to analyze and understand the general factors and their interrelationships that lead teachers' decisions on how to prevent school violence. Bronfenbrenner (1979) suggested that the educational environment has four interrelated systems: microsystem, mesosystem, exosystem, and macrosystem (for a more detailed discussion of this theory, see chapter 4 of this book).

Table 5.1. Effective School Violence Prevention Strategies

Ecological Level	Definition	Example(s)	Strategies
Microsystem	Concerned with self	Student Teacher Parent	• Paths I can problem solve
Mesosystem	Concerned with self and others	Teacher–student Teacher–parent	• Cooperative learning • STEP • Good behavior game
Exosystem	Concerned with relationships among self, others	Teacher–parent–student Administration–teacher–student	• Seattle Social Development Project • Bullying Prevention Program
Macrosystem	Concerned with relationships among self, others, and various influencing factors	Teacher–parent–student–community	• Midwestern Prevention Project • Quantum Opportunities Program • Wraparound

U.S. Surgeon General's Violence Report (2001).

At the microsystem level, prevention techniques that focus on the "self" (such as the student or teacher) will be delineated and described. Next will be a discussion on the mesosystem, which consists of the interrelations among teachers and students and teachers and parents. The exosystem takes into consideration school violence prevention techniques that are based on student–teacher–parent and administration–teacher–student relationships. Finally, prevention/intervention strategies that consider the student–parent–teacher–community or the macrosystem level will be discussed. It is proposed that no single intervention is effective when presented in an isolated format. In this proposed school prevention model, it is assumed that the relationship between each variable is complex.

Microsystem

School-based interventions at the microsystem level include moral reasoning, problem solving, and thinking skills. These three strategies were cited as best practices by the U.S. Surgeon General (2001) for reducing youth violence in high-risk populations. Social-skills training programs such as Promoting Alternative Thinking Strategies (PATHS) and I Can Problem Solve were found to have positive effects for reducing risk factors associated with violence. PATHS is taught to children in the kindergarten through 6th grade. The program promotes emotional competence through expression, understanding, and regulations of emotions. Self-control, social competence, positive peer relations, and interpersonal problem-solving skills are also taught. The purpose of these sessions is for students to learn new skills and generalize these skills in daily events. Evaluations of PATHS show that this program has improved behavior in regular education students and students with hyperactivity, peer aggression, and misconduct.

I Can Problem Solve serves as an effective violence-prevention program for children in nursery school, kindergarten, and grades 5 and 6. This program trains children to use problem-solving skills to find solutions to interpersonal problems. It is considered a cognitive approach in that it teaches children how to think. They learn that behavior causes something, that people have feelings, and that there are multiple ways to solve problems. According to Sochet (2000), "as they learn to associate how they think with what they can do, children become more caring and better able to share, cooperate, and get along with others" (27).

Similarly, the Anger Coping Program, a thinking-skills and social-skills training intervention, provides cognitive behavioral training to children 8 to 14 years old. The program consists of direct modeling, role-playing, group problem solving, and positive reinforcement activities to small groups of five to seven children. Research results report large reductions in disruptive-aggressive behavior immediately after the program's completion.

Mesosystem

School-based interventions identified at the mesosystem level focusing on teacher–student relationships included classroom behavior management. For example, the *Good Behavior Game*, designed for elementary school children, seeks to reduce early aggressive and shy behaviors. At the beginning of the game, teachers assign students to teams consisting of aggressive, disruptive, and shy children. The team's work is a collaborative effort among all members. The teacher identifies and defines a set of disruptive behaviors and if any member in the team engages in the disruptive behavior, the team receives a check. At the end of the game, the team not exceeding the amount of designated checks receives a tangible reward or activity. Since one of the goals is to modify shy behavior, shy children are appointed as the team leader with the responsibility of handling rewards. The evaluation of this program, as rated by teachers, has shown a positive effect for 1st-grade boys and girls on reducing aggressive and shy behaviors. Long-term treatment effects for participants in the program who were males identified as aggressive in the 1st grade showed a decrease in aggression in the 6th grade. The School Transitional Environmental Program (STEP) was another classroom-management program identified by the U.S. Surgeon General as effective for reducing substance use and delinquency while improving academic achievement and lowering school dropout rates. This program aims at reducing stress and disorganization often associated with transitioning from one school to another, which places children at risk of maladaptive behavior. Classroom management is used to create an environment that promotes academic achievement and to reduce school behavior problems and absenteeism.

Compensatory education strategies, such as adult tutoring, involve pulling students out of their regular classes to receive extra assistance in reading or math. This strategy is considered effective for improving academic performance for students at risk of failure. Moreover, when older children tutor younger children both groups have shown academic gain (U.S. Surgeon General 2001).

Two additional teaching strategies that were identified as primary prevention strategies effective for reducing at-risk academic failure and risk factors for youth violence are continuous progress and cooperative learning. Continuous progress, also referred to as looping, is a strategy that allows students to master a set of skills and then advance to the next level. This approach promotes continuity between teachers and students. It also allows students to maintain a caring, connected relationship with teachers. Perhaps the success of this intervention stems from the fact that it meets the child's educational needs and at the same time establishes and maintains an adult relationship. Cooperative learning is a strategy that affords an opportunity for students to work collaboratively with their peers in a small group. Research has shown the positive effect on improving attitudes about race relations, students with special needs, and overall attitudes about school.

Exosystem

School-based interventions that are concerned with relationships between self and others (e.g., teacher–student–parent) can also be found in behavior management programs. According to the U.S. Surgeon General, behavioral approach strategies are effective for reducing youth violence, delinquency, and related risk factors. For example, the Behavioral Monitoring and Reinforcement Program (Bry 1982, as cited in the U.S. Surgeon General 2001) focuses on adolescents who are characterized as having delinquency and substance abuse, including low motivation for school, disregard for rules, and feelings of alienation from parents. This program has four components: (a) weekly report cards, (b) discussion of report cards, (c) parent contact, and (d) follow-up sessions. The weekly report is completed based on teacher interviews about student behavior in the classroom, such as bringing materials to class, tardiness, and work completion. Students receive praise when they receive a positive report and redirection on how to improve their behavior if they receive a negative report. Parents are kept apprised of their child's progress via phone calls, letters, and home visits. Follow-up sessions, following the same format, occur two years after the intervention. Research studies conducted on this program, which focuses on enhancing positive student behavior, attendance, and academic achievement through consistent rewards and monitoring, was found to reduce substance abuse, self-reported criminal activity, and arrests, as well as enhance academic achievement in middle school students. In one study, for example, students exposed to this type of intervention were far less likely than students in a control group to have a delinquency record five years after the program.

The Seattle Social Development Project is another example of a program that focuses on teacher–student–parent connections and uses classroom behavior management among its core components. The aim of this model program is to reduce childhood risk factors for delinquency and drug abuse while fostering positive bonds between the child, family, and school. The project included individual and environmental changes known to help prevent violence, such as classroom management, team teaching, and peer buddies for students having different abilities and backgrounds. In addition, parents received training on how to monitor their child's behavior and use positive reinforcement. According to the U.S. Surgeon General, the components of the Seattle Social Development Program which targeted prosocial behavior such as interpersonal problem solving, academic success, and avoidance of drug use, reduced the initiation of alcohol, marijuana, and tobacco use by grade 6 and improved attachment and commitment to school. Furthermore, at age 18, youths who participated in the full five-year version of this program had lower rates of violence, heavy drinking, and sexual activity (including multiple sexual partners and pregnancy) and better academic performance than controls. The Bullying Prevention Program, designed for elementary and middle schools, is a promising program that begins with an anonymous student questionnaire designed to determine bullying problems. Based on the results of the questionnaire, parents, teachers, and students implement school, classroom, and individual-level interventions. This program reinforces the development of positive, caring connections. It was noted in one study, that after two years of this program in elementary and middle schools in Bergen, Norway, bullying problems decreased by 50 percent. Similar results have been reported in England, Germany, and the United States.

According to the U.S. Surgeon General, programs that target families of high-risk children are among the most effective in preventing violence. Several family-based, school-focused strategies and programs identified by the U.S. Surgeon General, such as the Linking the Interests of Families and Teachers (LIFT), the Incredible Years Series, and the Montreal Longitudinal Study (Preventive Treatment Program) are included and described in chapter 6.

Macrosystem

Three interventions—Quantum Opportunities Program, Wraparound, and Midwestern Prevention Projects—were identified that require involvement from students, teachers, parents, and other influencing factors, such as the community. The Quantum Opportunities Program is a community-based intervention designed for disadvantaged adolescents. Students who participate in this program are assigned to a peer group and a caring adult. The relationships are established during the 9th grade and continue throughout the high school years. The program provides an opportunity for educational, developmental, and service activities. For example, students have up to 250 hours of educational services to enhance academic skills. This is an after-school program designed to keep high-risk youth in high school and ultimately attend college by improving their academic skills.

Wraparound programs provide comprehensive services based on a child's individual needs. It is a systematic approach that takes into consideration the child, the family, and the caregivers. Research results have shown reductions in recidivism and arrest rates during the year following participation.

The Midwestern Prevention Project focuses on middle school children and its goal is to reduce substance abuse associated with the developmental period between early adolescence and late adolescence. The program trains youth to avoid drug use and heighten their awareness of when drugs are likely to be used. This project has demonstrated the ability to reduce drug usage for participants.

CONCLUSION

This chapter describes prevention/intervention strategies based on the premise of an ethic of care (Noddings 1984) and an ecological framework (Bronfenbrenner 1979). Implementing school violence prevention strategies based on these theories will not be an easy task. It is necessary, therefore, to summarize ways presented in this chapter for adapting an ethic of care and ecological perspective. One possible way is for children to make positive caring connections with adults. Noddings suggests that there are ways to extend contact with students, such as teachers working with their students for an extended period of time. This strategy, known as continuous progress or looping, has been identified by the U.S. Surgeon General and the U.S. Secret Service as a very effective way to prevent violence. It is believed that this type of continuity would be beneficial for two reasons. First, it allows time to establish a relationship, and second, it allows for continuity in the curriculum.

For this to be accomplished, universities must be responsible for preparing teachers to become caring adults. Reforms in teacher education have focused on preparing teachers who will increase academic success, adding to teacher knowledge bases and eliminating teacher-candidates who do not meet minimum requirements (Noddings 1984; Rogers and Webb 1991). Little attention has been given to increasing caring behaviors in prospective teachers, yet Noddings (1984) suggests that such focus would serve to increase academic outcomes for students. Perhaps little attention has been given to increasing caring behaviors in teacher education because it is not well defined, not well examined, and not well articulated (Rogers & Webb 1991). Smith and Emigh (1999) believe that new teachers will model the relationships they have during teacher education when they enter their own classrooms. It would seem then that the characteristics of caring need to be implemented by professors involved in teacher education.

REFERENCES

Ascher, C. 1994. *Gaining control over violence in the schools*. East Lansing, MI: National Center for Research on Teacher Learning. (ERIC Document Reproduction Service No. ED 377 256)

Barr, R. D., and W. H. Parrett. 2001. *Hope fulfilled for at-risk and violent youth, K–12 programs that work*. Boston: Allyn and Bacon.

Bronfenbrenner, U. 1979. *The ecology of human development: Experiments in nature and design*. Cambridge, Mass.: Harvard University Press.

Collinson, V., M. Killeavy, and H. J. Stephenson. 1999. Exemplary teachers: Practicing an ethic of care in England, Ireland, and the United States. *Journal for a Just and Caring Education* 5(4): 349–60.

Daly, P. M. 1985. Lesson from ten years of teacher improvement reform. *Educational Leadership* 52(5): 26–32.

Eisner, E. W. 1997. The new frontier in qualitative research methodology. *Qualitative Inquiry* 3(3): 259–73.

Hamilton Fish Institute. 2000. *Guns in schools,* at www.hamfish.org/about/pr091400.php3 (accessed December 4, 2001).

Harrington-Lueker, D. 2001. Middle schools fail to make the grade. *USA Today,* March 15, A15.

Hyman, I. A., and P. A. Snook. 2000. Dangerous schools and what you can do about them. *Phi Delta Kappan* 81(7): 489–501.

Jenson, J. M., and M. O. Howard. 1999. *Youth violence: Current research and recent practice innovations.* Washington, D.C.: National Association of Social Workers Press.

Kantrowitz, B., and P. Wingert. May 10, 1999. How well do you know your kid? *Newsweek* 133(19): 36–40.

Kratzer, C. C. 1996. *Beyond "effective school research": Cultivating a caring community in an urban school.* Paper presented at the annual meeting of the American Educational Research Association, New York. (ERIC Document Reproduction Services ED 397 211)

Lambert, N. S. 1995. *Perspectives of successful teachers reputed as caring: Explanations for connection in the classroom.* Unpublished doctoral dissertation, University of South Florida, Tampa.

Linkous, V. D. 1989. Patterns of caring: A study of the perceptions of teachers and students (Doctoral dissertation, Virginia Polytechnic Institute and State University 1989). *Dissertation Abstracts International,* 50, 07A, p. 1920.

Metropolitan Life Insurance Company. 2000. *The Metropolitan Life survey of the American teacher, 2000: Are we preparing students for the 21st century?* New York: Louis Harris.

Morse, W. C. 1994. The role of caring in teaching children with behavior problems. *Contemporary Education* 65(3): 132–36.

National Association of Secondary Principals. 1996. Breaking ranks: Changing an American institution. A report of the national association of secondary school principals on the high school of the twenty-first century. *NASSP Bulletin* 80(578): 55–66.

National School Safety Center. 2000. *School associated violent deaths,* at www.nssc1.org (accessed December 4, 2001).

Noblit, G. W. 1993. Power and caring. *American Educational Research Journal* 30(1): 23–38.

Noddings, N. 1984. *Caring: A feminine approach to ethics and moral education.* Berkeley: University of California Press.

Noddings, N. 1991. Stories in dialogue: Caring and interpersonal reasoning. In *Stories lives tell: Narrative and dialogue in education,* ed. C. Witherell and N. Noddings, pp. 157–70. New York: Teachers College Press.

Noddings, N. 1992. *The challenge to care in schools: An alternate approach to education.* New York: Teachers College Press.

Noddings, N. 1995. Teaching themes of care. *Phi Delta Kappan* 76(9): 675–79.

Office of Juvenile Justice and Delinquency Prevention. 1999. *Violence after school,* at www.ojjdp.ncjrs.org (accessed December 4, 2001).

Phelan, P., A. L. Davidson, and H. T. Cao. 1992. Speaking up: Students' perspectives on school. *Phi Delta Kappan* 73(9): 689–704.

Resnick, M. D., P. S. Bearman, R. W. Blum, K. E. Bauman, K. M. Harris, J. Johnes, T. Tabor, T. Beuhring, R. E. Sieving, M. Shew, M. Ireland, L. H. Bearinger, and J. R. Udry. 1997. Protecting adolescents from harm: Findings from the national longitudinal study on adolescent health. *Journal of American Medical Association* 287(10): 823–32.

Rogers, D., and J. Webb. 1991. The ethic of caring in teacher education. *Journal of Teacher Education* 42(3): 173–81.

Siddle-Walker, E. V. 1993. Interpersonal caring in the "good" segregated schooling of African American children: Evidence from the case of Casewell County training school. *The Urban Review* 25(1): 63–77.

Skiba, R. J., and R. L. Peterson. 2000. School discipline at a crossroad: From zero tolerance to early response. *Exceptional Children* 66(3): 335–47.

Smith, R. L., and L. Emigh. 1999. *A model for defining the construct of caring in teacher education.* Unpublished manuscript, University of South Florida, Sarasota.

Sochet, M. 2000. *The nuts and bolts of implementing school safety programs.* New York: Vera Institute of Justice.

U.S. Department of Education. 1998. *Turn around low-performing schools: A guide for state and local leaders.* Washington, D.C.: Author.

U.S. Department of Education and Department of Justice. 2000. *Annual report on school safety,* at www.ed.gov/offices/OESE/SDF/annrept00.pdf (accessed February 22, 2002).

U.S. Secret Service and U.S. Department of Education. 2002. *Implications for the prevention of school attacks in the United States.* The final report and findings of the safe school initiative, at www.secretservice.gov/ntac/ntac_ssi_report.pdf (accessed February 22, 2002).

U.S. Surgeon General. 2001. Youth violence: A report of the Surgeon General. Rockville, MD: U.S. Department of Health and Human Services, Centers for Disease Control and Prevention, National Center for Inquiry Prevention and Control, Substance Abuse and Mental Health Services Administration, Center for Mental Health Services, and National Institutes of Health, National Institute of Mental Health.

Van Galen, J. A. 1996. Caring community: The limitations of compassion in facilitating diversity. In *Caring in an unjust world: Negotiating borders and barriers in schools,* ed. D. Eaker-Rich and J. A. Van Galen. Albany: State University of New York Press.

Chapter Six

Family Programs to Help Reduce Violence

Karen B. Clark

The family is clearly at the center of both Bronfenbrenner's ecological model and Noddings's ethics of care model. In both, the family provides the developmental environment for a child. This early environment, including the interactions among caregivers, infants, and children, can have a significant effect on the development of social competence (Loeber and Stouthamer-Loeber 1986). Home environments that are most likely to produce positive social behaviors have been described by Eisenberg and Fabes (1998) as warm, affectionate, and nurturing—the opposite of home environments where children exhibit violent and aggressive behaviors.

Beyond providing nurturing environments, families may contribute to a child's positive social development by exhibiting certain behaviors (Mussen and Eisenberg 2001). Adult behaviors considered to be related to prosocial behaviors in children include reasoning to influence children's behavior and promote moral development (Hoffman 1970), modeling caring behaviors (Eisenberg and Fabes 1998), and using attributional praise to reinforce positive behaviors (Grusec and Redler 1980). Indeed, such behaviors seem to have a central place in Noddings's ethics of care model.

However, not all families engage in behaviors that produce positive social behavior in children. Even families who do demonstrate these desirable behaviors may experience circumstances that temporarily decrease these positive behaviors or change the generally positive milieu of the home. In such cases where family interactions do not—or temporarily cannot—promote prosocial behaviors, it may be critical for other agencies, such as community organizations or schools, to become involved in providing services to families to enhance the home environment and social competence of children.

The purpose of this chapter is to present information about family programs designed to enhance home environments and decrease violent or antisocial behavior in children and youth. First, information about family-based programs reviewed by the U.S. Surgeon General (2001) will be presented. This will be followed by recommendations for forming caring family–school partnerships to promote prosocial behaviors and academic success in children. Finally, it will conclude with an overview of federal legislation and suggested policies that may have an indirect effect on the behavior of children.

FAMILY-BASED PROGRAMS RECOMMENDED BY THE SURGEON GENERAL

In January 2001, the U.S. Surgeon General issued a report on youth violence. The immediate impetus for the report was the Columbine High School shootings that occurred in April 1999. The report summarized research related to school violence and, more important, presented information on programs that could be implemented to reduce the occurrence of future violence.

One of the conclusions from the report is that targeting families of high-risk children and families with children who are already engaging in violent actions may have the biggest impact on preventing future violent behavior (U.S. Surgeon General 2001). In evaluating prevention and intervention programs for families, the Surgeon General categorized programs in three ways: (a) model, (b) promising, or (c) ineffective. Model programs are those that have been examined using a rigorous experimental or quasi-experimental design, been found to have significant deterrent effects, been replicated in a variety of sites, and been found to have sustainable results. Promising programs fit the first two criteria for design and effect, and either have been replicated or have sustainable results, but not both. The following sections, organized according to the ages of the children in the target families, review some of these model and promising programs.

PROMISING EARLY INTERVENTION
PROGRAMS FOR FAMILIES

The Family Development Research Program at Syracuse University began by serving young, impoverished mothers during their last trimester of pregnancy. It included weekly home visits by paraprofessionals who encouraged positive parent–child interactions and healthful home environments. The weekly visitors also helped mothers secure necessary services. In addition, the program provided four years of quality day care for infants beginning at 6 months old (Zigler and Styfco 2001).

The Yale Child Welfare Research Program also began working with mothers during the prenatal period. The intent of the program was to help mothers secure services that might relieve stressing factors thereby allowing them to engage in more effective child-rearing practices (Zigler and Styfco 2001). This program served young mothers who were trying to raise their first-born infants in a high-risk environment. The program served these mothers during the prenatal period and lasted about thirty months. Agents tried to help mothers secure social work services, and medical and psychological services, along with providing high-quality child care (Zigler and Styfco 2001).

The High Scope/Perry Preschool is an early intervention program that is familiar to many because of its long evaluation period. Its preschool graduates were 27 years old when data were last collected to assess the long-term effects of the program (Zigler and Styfco 2001). The Perry Preschool provided early childhood education to young children for two years. In addition, its teachers visited mothers weekly to assist them with efforts to carry out the curriculum at home. Long-term benefits of the program for participants include higher graduation and employment rates, and lower reliance on welfare programs (Berreuta-Clement et al. 1984). In addition, male graduates of the program had lower arrest rates than those in the control group (Zigler and Styfco 2001).

A fourth promising early intervention program is the Incredible Years Program (Reid and Webster-Stratton 2001). This program is described as multicontextual because it addresses the needs and interactions between parents, teachers, and children during the preschool and school-age years. The program is designed to promote prosocial skills while reducing conduct problems in children beginning at age 3. In each of the curricular areas,

trainers use videotapes to enhance parent involvement with schools, improve classroom teachers' classroom management skills, and teach children
social skills, empathy, anger management, and conflict resolution.

The success of these programs highlights the importance of early intervention with children and families in preventing violence. All four programs are comprehensive and connected, involving families, children, and
early interventionists in an effort to promote positive behavior at an early
age. Because not all families are eligible for early intervention programs,
or may choose not to participate in them, it is important to be familiar with
programs that target school-age children and families. The next section of
this chapter reviews promising programs for this age group.

PROMISING PROGRAMS FOR SCHOOL-AGE CHILDREN, YOUTH, AND FAMILIES

Linking the Interests of Families and Teachers (LIFT) is a program that has
been researched by Reid et al. (2000). Their study involves 1st- through
5th-grade students and their families, and combines school-based skills
training for children with parent training. The school-based skills training
for students is designed to promote developmentally appropriate social
skills. A peer component of the program focuses on encouraging positive
social behavior and eliminating physical aggression during playground activities. The third component of LIFT is parent training. As part of this
component, parent groups meet to discuss consistent limit setting and to
encourage parent involvement in the child's social activities. Children who
participate in LIFT exhibit less physical aggression on the playground, better social skills, and, in the long term, less likelihood of associating with
delinquent peers, using alcohol, or being arrested (Reid et al. 2001).

A second program for school-age youth, and evaluated as a promising
program, is titled the Preventive Treatment Program or the Montreal Longitudinal Study. This program is aimed at preventing delinquency among
disruptive 7- to 9-year-old boys from low-income families. The program
has two aspects: school-based social skills training and parent training.
The parent training sessions teach parents to read with their children,
monitor and reinforce behavior, use effective methods of discipline, and
manage family crises (Tremblay et al. 1996).

The next three programs target families with middle school students. The Iowa Strengthening Families Program targets youth between the ages of 10 and 14 and their families. It consists of seven weekly sessions of parent and child training designed to improve parenting skills and family communication. The sessions typically include a variety of activities such as discussions of videotapes portraying negative and positive interactions between youth and parents, gamelike skill-building activities specifically for youth, and family sessions with discussions, games, and projects (Molgaard and Spoth 2001). Studies show that students participating in the program demonstrate fewer conduct problems in school and that the skills gained have greater positive effects for sustained periods of time.

Another middle school program, Preparing for the Drug-Free Years, is for parents with children in grades 4 through 8. It is designed to prevent drug use and behavior problems by strengthening parenting skills and family bonding. One session on peer pressure includes both students and parents, while the remaining sessions include only parents (Kosterman et al. 2001).

The Surgeon General's report describes Families and Schools Together (FAST) as the most comprehensive program implemented in multiple contexts. The program originally targeted children identified as disruptive during the elementary years, but now is used with middle school youth (McDonald and Sayger 1998). FAST develops separate support networks for youth and their parents. The program addresses factors related to school failure, violence, delinquency, and substance abuse in sessions where both youth and parents are active participants.

The five programs reviewed in this section show great promise for preventing aggression and other problematic behaviors with elementary and middle school students. Despite the success of these and other programs, some young people will still engage in destructive and antisocial behaviors. These students will need intensive interventions to change established behavior patterns and reduce the likelihood of recidivism. Therefore, two programs evaluated as model family clinical interventions are discussed in the next section.

MODEL FAMILY CLINICAL INTERVENTIONS

Tremblay and Craig (1995) suggest that marital and family therapy have a positive effect on several aspects of family life, including child behavior and delinquency. Two programs classified by the Surgeon General as model programs following a family therapy approach are Functional Family Therapy and Multisystemic Therapy.

Functional Family Therapy (FFT) targets youth between 11 and 18 years of age (Alexander and Parsons 1982; Sexton and Alexander 2000). Youth who participate are at-risk of or are already demonstrating problematic behaviors. FFT is an integrated intervention model that is implemented in phases and across a variety of settings. Its approach incorporates family therapy based on social learning theory and a focus on the function of certain behaviors within the family structure (Horne 1993). It includes eight to thirty hours of direct services for youth and families. Two of the services focus on behavior change resulting from direct skills training with youth and parents. These services also provide opportunities to generalize this training to the home environment to ensure that the new skills are related to authentic family needs. FFT is one model that has the support of empirical research documenting its effectiveness with aggressive children involved with juvenile gang activity (Horne 1993).

Multisystemic Therapy (MST) is a more intensive family- and community-based treatment program that targets families with children already being served by the juvenile justice system for violence or substance abuse (Henggeler, Melton, and Smith 1992). Services consist of strategic family therapy, structural family therapy, behavioral parent training, and cognitive behavioral therapy. The amount of time families spend in MST depends on the youth and family needs.

One final approach to working with youth in a variety of contexts is known as a wraparound approach. A wraparound approach is based on a system of care and involves building on the strengths of the student, family, and care providers. Wraparound teams consist of family members, teachers, other school personnel, and representatives of community agencies. The resulting plans are extensive, flexible, and are designed to meet the needs of students and families beyond the school day (Eber, Nelson, and Miles 1997). Plans are comprehensive enough to address issues such as family residence, psychological and medical needs, community safety, cultural backgrounds, and financial services.

Wraparound services are often used with children and youth identified as having emotional or behavioral disorders (EBD). Research examining the implementation of wraparound services in the state of Illinois suggests that wraparound services provide many benefits including a reduction in the number of restrictive placements for EBD youth, improvements in overall classroom performance, and behavior improvements in unsupervised settings (Eber et al. 1997). The wraparound approach, with children and families at its center, is rooted in Bronfenbrenner's ecological model (Duckworth et al. 2001).

These three comprehensive programs are encouraging interventions for children and youth at risk for or already engaged in antisocial behaviors. Beyond these programs that address the needs of specific students, schools might be advised to routinely engage in practices that form meaningful partnerships with families. Such partnerships may promote positive attitudes toward school as well as enhance prosocial behaviors. The next section discusses practices that encourage families to routinely be involved in the education of their children.

SCHOOL AND FAMILY PARTNERSHIPS

Noddings (1995) suggests that care is demonstrated in many ways. School and family partnerships demonstrate care by cooperating in children's activities and by providing favorable conditions that foster positive child development. When such caring partnerships are formed, school achievement might be enhanced (Graue, Weinstein, and Walberg 1983) and negative behaviors can be reduced (Wang, Haertel, and Walberg 1993). However, for school-family partnerships to have positive results, schools must consider the needs of contemporary families and youth, which may result in changes to some traditional school practices that involve families.

TRADITIONAL SCHOOL PRACTICES
AND FAMILY INVOLVEMENT

Traditional practices that lead to family involvement with schools include inviting parents to attend PTA meetings, holding parent–teacher conferences, distributing report cards, communicating with parents when there is a concern or something to celebrate, asking parents to engage in fundraising or volunteer activities, requesting that parents facilitate homework completion, inviting parents to performances, and including parents on committees that review school policies. Many of these opportunities are designed to involve parents, and positive interactions with schools and positive partnerships may result. For example, participating in a parent–teacher conference when positive student progress is being reported is a welcome experience for most parents. Parents leave the conference feeling that they have a positive connection or relationship with the school and its professionals. However, the conference may have the opposite result. For example, the parent–teacher conference that focuses on lack of student achievement or poor behavior is likely to leave a parent feeling angry or alienated. The parents wonder why they were not notified of the problem sooner and leave the school feeling estranged from the school community. The long-term result is that the parents become either complacent or combative, neither leading to an effective partnership.

Within the past several years, educators have suggested replacing traditional practices with family-centered (Hammond 1999) or family-friendly practices (Epstein 1995). These newer activities offer more promise than some traditional efforts at positively involving parents in innovative and meaningful ways in the education of their children.

CURRENT SCHOOL–FAMILY PARTNERSHIPS

The early intervention literature provides some descriptions of family-centered practices. Murphy et al. describe family-centered practices as those which "(a) include families in decision-making, planning, assessment, and service delivery at family, agency, and systems levels; (b) develop services for the whole family and not just the child; (c) are guided by families' priorities for goals and services; (d) offer and respect families' choices regarding the level of their participation" (as cited in Hammond 1999, 42). Given this description, family-centered practices take a more holistic view of families and students.

Comer (1984) was one of the first educators to involve families in innovative ways in his School Development Program initiated in New Haven, Connecticut. Comer's approach requires involving parents on school advisory councils and employing parents to assist in classrooms. Beyond this a mental health team is available in "Comer schools" to support children, staff, and families.

Success for All out of Johns Hopkins University (Cooper, Slavin, and Madden 1998) is another program that solicits the active involvement of parents by providing a family support team consisting of social workers, attendance monitors, and a parent liaison. The parent team provides families with daily assistance with nutrition, medical needs, and problem behaviors. Family support teams also try to connect families to helpful community resources.

Dryfoos's (1994) full-service schools model is a comprehensive approach to meeting the complex needs of students and families. Full-service schools house clinics to meet the health, mental health, and social needs of their constituents. The clinics and services located in full-service schools vary according to identified needs and the acceptability of services to the school system and community.

More recently, Epstein (1995) has written extensively about creating school, family, and community partnerships. She writes, "The way schools care about children is reflected in the way schools care about the children's families" (701). Furthermore, Epstein suggests that such partnerships must be "family-friendly," meaning they are planned and based on the needs of the family and the realities of family life.

Epstein outlines six types of family–school partnerships: (a) parenting: helping all families establish home environments to support children as students; (b) communicating: designing effective two-way channels for school-to-home and home-to-school communications; (c) volunteering: recruiting and organizing parent help and support from a wide variety of families; (d) learning at home: providing information and ideas to family about interactive homework and other activities; (e) decision-making: including parents from all racial, ethnic, socioeconomic, and other groups in school decisions, and developing parental leadership; and (f) collaborating with community: integrating community resources and services to strengthen school programs and family practices. Such "family-friendly" practices redefine traditional school practices for involving families and replace them with a more "balanced, comprehensive program of partnerships" (Epstein 1995, 707). Interestingly, Epstein characterizes her six types of parent involvement as "six types of caring" (Epstein 2001, 408).

Epstein has implemented her philosophy of "family-friendly" partnerships by establishing the National Network of Partnership Schools (NNPS) in 1996. This organization provides guidance to schools attempting to inform and involve all families about their children's learning and development. The approach of NNPS is based on the belief that parents, teachers, and students must view each other as partners and form a caring community that ultimately benefits our nation's youth. The next section, in an effort to attain the goal of forming meaningful partnerships, discusses several policy initiatives, some from the NNPS.

THE ECOLOGICAL MODEL AND POLICY DECISIONS

The preceding sections of this chapter have focused on enhancing prosocial behavior through programs that are designed to improve family interactions and family environments. When such programs are limited to the involvement of children and families, they are within Bronfenbrenner's microsystem. When programs involve the interaction of schools, children, and families, they are within Bronfenbrenner's mesosystem. While these two inner circles of the ecological model have the most direct effect on children and youth, it is also important to examine policy decisions that affect children, families, and schools. Such policy decisions do not directly involve children, but may have an effect on their opportunities to participate in caring environments and, therefore, develop appropriate behaviors. The final section of this chapter examines the exosystem of Bronfenbrenner's model and discusses the potential effect of government legislation, workplace policies, teacher education, and school curriculum decisions on families and student behavior in schools.

POLICY INITIATIVES, FAMILY–SCHOOL PARTNERSHIPS, AND STUDENT BEHAVIOR

The relationship among policy initiatives, family–school partnerships, and student behavior is complex and difficult to measure. Unlike the family programs reviewed by the U.S. Surgeon General, it is difficult to categorize policy decisions as model, promising, or ineffective. However, several pieces of legislation have started a trend that acknowledges the importance of strong family partnerships. The following section explores some federal initiatives and recommendations.

FEDERAL POLICY INITIATIVES FOR
FAMILY–SCHOOL PARTNERSHIPS

Several federal pieces of legislation emerged during the 1990s that started a movement toward establishing family–school partnerships. In 1993–1994, President Clinton introduced Goals 2000: Educate America Act. It included promoting the idea of parental involvement as an important contributor to successful schools. Specifically, it provided for the creation of family information and resource centers along with parent representation on state and local school improvement panels.

The Elementary and Secondary Education Act (ESEA) was most recently reauthorized and signed into law by President Bush as the Leave No Child Behind Act of 2001. This legislation is a comprehensive set of laws designed to improve education, particularly educational equity. Title I is part of the ESEA and requires schools and states to include parents in planning, designing, and implementing local Title I programs. Under Title V of the ESEA, funding is provided to schools and community organizations to establish family information and resource centers for the purpose of establishing stronger family–school partnerships. Finally, the ESEA's Safe and Drug-Free Schools and Communities Act provides funding to develop and disseminate materials about the prevention of school violence.

The Individuals with Disabilities Education Act (IDEA) was most recently reauthorized in 1997 and is scheduled to be reviewed by Congress again in 2002. This major piece of legislation guarantees specific rights and protections related to the provision of appropriate educational programs to students with various disabilities. The act requires family-centered practices for meeting the needs of infants and toddlers as well as mandating parental involvement in all aspects of designing, implementing, and evaluating programs for school-age children and youth with disabilities.

Goals 2000, the ESEA or Leave No Child Behind Act of 2001, and the IDEA are three examples of federal legislation emphasizing the importance of family involvement in educational decision making. As a result of this federal legislation several states have also enacted their own initiatives for promoting stronger family and school alliances. Epstein (2001) provides an overview of several state and district policies that have the potential to establish strong school–family partnerships. Epstein's book *School, Family, and Community Partnerships* is an excellent resource for those beginning to identify promising practices in this area.

WORKPLACE POLICIES

In addition to federal and state legislation supporting family–school partnerships, some employers have also adopted practices and policies that promote partnerships between schools and families. Some suggestions for effective workplace policies can be found in the federal publication, *Strong Families/Strong Schools* (U.S. Department of Education 1994). Four suggestions are offered to employers for assisting families to form strong relationships with children and schools. The first suggestion for employers is to offer employees work flex-time. Flex-time typically requires employees to work core hours and then provides the flexibility to extend those hours according to specific family needs. Ideally, flex-time would facilitate parent participation in a variety of school events. Other suggestions for family-friendly policies include providing parent-training at job sites, offering libraries containing parenting materials, scheduling literacy training opportunities for families, and establishing family resource hot lines.

In addition to providing families with information and time to attend school-related events, the U.S. Department of Education (1994) also suggests providing family employees with high-quality child care options. Employers might consider providing on-site child care centers that would allow for convenient and frequent interactions with children and their family members. If this is not a possibility, it is recommended that businesses consider becoming involved with funding community child care centers or providing employers with vouchers to assist with expenses related to high-quality programs.

Finally, the last suggestion from the U.S. Department of Education is for businesses to form direct partnerships with schools. Such partnerships may allow and encourage employees to volunteer in schools, to participate in mentoring programs, to fund special projects or equipment, and to participate in school-to-work programs.

TEACHER EDUCATION AND
FAMILY–SCHOOL PARTNERSHIPS

Forming effective partnerships between schools and families often depends upon an individual teacher's ability to establish a collaborative relationship with a parent or care provider. Collaboration, as described by Friend and Cook (2000), is based on the assumptions that such interactions are (a) voluntary, (b) based on parity of participants, (c) designed to focus on mutual goals, (d) based on a philosophy of shared responsibility and decision making, and (e) based on the ability to share resources and accountability. Teacher education programs are including more classes in collaboration to meet the Interstate New Teacher Assessment and Support Consortium (INTASC) principles (Darling-Hammond, Wise, and Klein 1999). Of these ten principles that guide teacher education programs, principles 9 and 10 specifically refer to working with parents. They read as follows:

> Principle 9: The teacher is a reflective practitioner who continually evaluates the effects of his/her choices and actions on others (students, parents, and other professionals in the learning community) and who actively seeks out opportunities to grow professionally.
>
> Principle 10: The teacher fosters relationships with school colleagues; parents, and agencies in the larger community to support students' learning and well-being. (Darling-Hammond et al. 1999, 187)

Other professional organizations also have separate but often related standards that refer to a teacher's ability to collaborate with families. Such principles that serve to guide programs preparing future educators can only result in stronger, more effective school–family partnerships.

CURRICULUM AND SCHOOL ORGANIZATION

While the main topic of this chapter is family programs to reduce violence, it is important to consider the organization of schools and the design of curriculum as it relates to the behavior of students. Much of our current educational policy focuses on maintaining high academic standards, ensuring that teachers are prepared to help students attain those standards, and implementing measures for state and school accountability systems. Some would suggest that in this present climate it will be difficult to organize schools as models of care (Noddings 1995). However, some current trends related to curriculum and school organization do seem to suggest that many schools are striving to provide caring and nurturing environments for children and youth.

Some promising structures include creating schools that are smaller with family-type groupings (Hunt 2002). Another structural change is the practice of "looping" or of allowing teachers and students to remain together for longer than the traditional academic year (Black 2000; Chirichello and Chirichello 2001). Finally, Noddings suggests organizing the curriculum itself around themes of care (Noddings 1995). Such themes might include (a) caring for self, (b) caring for intimate others, and (c) caring for strangers and global others. While such structural and curricular change may be difficult to implement, if the results included developing sensitive prosocial behaviors in our nation's youth and reducing violence, they could be well worth the effort.

CONCLUSION

The purpose of this chapter is to present information on family programs for enhancing home environments and positive behavior in children and youth, to provide suggestions for establishing meaningful family–school partnerships, and to discuss federal legislation with the potential to strengthen these partnerships. In addition, limited information is provided about possible school structures and curriculum initiatives that may promote more caring schools. Each of these issues is related to Bronfenbrenner's ecological model and Noddings's ethics of care model.

It is critical that both educators and parents be better informed about successful family interventions and the recommended practices for strengthening family–school partnerships. School and home environments, consistent with Bronfenbrenner's ecological model and Noddings's ethics of care model, have great effects on the behavior and social competence of children and youth. Beyond this, by creating caring environments, we may be able to enhance the overall quality of life for today's students as well as their future families.

REFERENCES

Alexander, J., and B. Parsons. 1973. Short-term behavioral interventions with delinquent families: Impact on family process and recidivism. *Abnormal Psychology* 81: 219–25.

Alexander, J., and B. Parsons. 1982. *Functional family therapy*. Pacific Grove, Calif.: Brooks/Cole.

Berreuta-Clement, J. R., L. Schweinhard, W. Barnett, A. Epstein, and D. Weikart. 1984. *Changed lives: The effects of the Perry Preschool Program on youths through age 19*. Ypsilante, Mich.: High/Scope Educational Research Foundation.

Black, S. 2000. Together again: The practice of looping keeps students with same teachers. *American School Board Journal* 187(6): 40–43.

Chirichello, M., and C. Chirechello. (2001). A standing ovation for looping. *Childhood Education* 78(1): 2–11.

Comer, J. 1984. *Improving American education: Roles for parents*. Hearing before the Select Committee on Children, Youth, and Families. Washington, D.C.: U.S. Government Printing Office.

Cooper, R., R. E. Slavin, and N. A. Madden. 1998. Success for all: Improving the quality of implementation of whole-school change through the use of a national reform network. *Education and Urban Society* 30(3): 385–429.

Darling-Hammond, L., A. E. Wise, and S. P. Klein. 1999. *A license to teach: Raising standards for teaching*. San Francisco: Jossey-Bass.

Dryfoos, J. G. 1994. *Full-service schools*. San Francisco: Jossey-Bass.

Duckworth, S., S. Smith-Rex, S. Okey, M. A. Brookshire, D. Rawlinson, R. Rawlinson, S. Castillo, and J. Little. 2001. Wraparound services for young schoolchildren with emotional and behavioral disorders. *Teaching Exceptional Children* 33(4): 54–60.

Eber, L., C. M. Nelson, and P. Miles. 1997. School-based wraparound for students with emotional and behavioral challenges. *Exceptional Children* 63(4): 539–55.

Eisenberg, N., and R. A. Fabes. 1998. Prosocial development. In *Handbook of child psychology: Volume 3. Social, emotional, and personality development*, ed. W. Damon and N. Eisenberg (5th ed.). New York: Wiley.

Epstein, J. L. 1995. School/family/community partnerships: Caring for the children we share. *Phi Delta Kappan* 76(9): 701–13.

Epstein, J. L. 2001. *School, family, and community partnerships, preparing educators and improving schools*. Boulder, Colo.: Westview Press.

Friend, M., and L. Cook. 2000. *Interactions, collaboration skills for school professionals* (3d ed.) New York: Addison Wesley Longman.

Graue, N. E., T. Weinstein, and H. J. Walberg. 1983. School-based home instruction and learning. A quantitative syntheses. *Journal of Educational Research* 76(6): 351–60.

Grusec, J. E., and E. Redler. 1980. Attribution, reinforcement and altruism: A developmental analysis. *Developmental Psychology* 16: 525–34.

Hammond, H. (1999). Identifying best family-centered practices in early-intervention programs. *Teaching Exceptional Children* 33(4): 42–46.

Henggeler, S. W., G. B. Melton, and L. A. Smith. 1992. Family preservation using multisystemic therapy: An effective alternative to incarcerating serious juvenile offenders. *Journal of Consulting and Clinical Psychology* 60(6): 953–61.

Hoffman, M. L. (1970). Conscience, personality, and socialization techniques. *Human Development* 13: 90–126.

Horne, A. M. 1993. Family-based interventions. In *The Gang Intervention Handbook,* ed. A. P. Goldstein and C. R. Huff. Champaign, Ill.: Research Press.

Hunt, J. B. (2002). Leadership in education: A view from the states. *Phi Delta Kappan* 83(9): 714–23.

Kosterman, R., J. D. Hawkins, K. P. Haggerty, R. Spoth, and C. Redmond. 2001. Preparing for the drug-free years: Session-specific effects of a universal parent-training program. *Journal of Drug Education* 31(1): 47–69.

Loeber, R., and M. Stouthamer-Loeber. 1987. Prediction. In *Handbook of Juvenile Delinquency,* ed. H. Quay. New York: Wiley.

McDonald, L., and T. Sayger. 1998. Impact of a family and school-based prevention program on protective factors for high-risk youth. *Drugs and Society* 12: 61–86.

Molgaard, V., and R. Spoth. 2001. Strengthening Families Program for young adolescents: Overview and outcomes. In *Innovative mental health programs for children,* ed. S. Pfeiffer and L. Reddy. Binghamton, N.Y.: Haworth Press.

Mussen, P., and N. Eisenberg. 2001. Prosocial development in context. In *Constructive & destructive behavior: Implications for family, school, and society,* ed. A. C. Bohart and D. J. Stipek. Washington, D.C.: American Psychological Association.

Noddings, N. 1995. Teaching themes of care. *Phi Delta Kappan* 76(9): 675–79.

Reid, J. B., J. M. Eddy, R. A. Fetrow, and M. Stoolmiller. 2000. Description and immediate impacts of a preventive intervention for conduct problems. *American Journal of Community Psychology* 27(4): 483–517.

Reid, M. J., and C. Webster-Stratton. 2001. The Incredible Years parent, teacher, and child intervention. Targeting multiple areas of risk for a young child with pervasive, conduct problems using a flexible manualized treatment program. *Journal of Cognitive and Behavior Practice* 8: 377–86.

Sexton, T. L., and Alexander, J. F. 2000, December. Functional family therapy. *OJJDP Juvenile Justice Bulletin*, 1–7.

Tremblay, R., and W. Craig. 1995. Developmental crime prevention. In *Building a safer society: Strategic approaches to crime prevention,* vol. 19, ed. M. Tonry and D. P. Farrington Chicago: University of Chicago Press.

Tremblay, R. E., L. Masse, L. Pagani, and F. Vitaro. 1996. From childhood physical aggression to adolescent maladjustment: The Montreal Prevention Experiment. In *Preventing childhood disorders, substance abuse, and delinquency,* ed. R. D. Peters and R. J. McMahon. Thousand Oaks, Calif.: Sage.

U.S. Department of Education. 1994. *Strong families, strong schools: Building community partnerships for learning. A research base for family involvement in learning.* ERIC Document Reproduction Services ED371909.

U.S. Surgeon General. 2001. *Youth violence: A report of the Surgeon General.* (DHHS Publication 451422). Washington, D.C.: U.S. Government Printing Office.

Wang, M. C., G. D. Haertel, and H. J. Walberg. 1993. Educational resilience in inner cities. In *Educational resilience in inner-city America. Challenges and prospects,* ed. M. C. Wang and E. W. Gordon. Hillsdale, N.J.: Lawrence Erlbaum.

Zigler, E., and S. J. Styfco. 2001. Can early childhood intervention prevent delinquency: A real possibility. In *Constructive and destructive behavior. Implications for family, school, and society,* ed. A. C. Bohart and D. J. Stipek. Washington, D.C.: American Psychological Association.

Chapter Seven

Community Violence Prevention/Intervention

Denise Smith

Community violence is increasingly invading the lives of children living in America, particularly those who live in socially disorganized areas. Socially disorganized neighborhoods are characterized as communities with high levels of crime, drug selling, gangs, poor housing, physical deterioration, and population density (Williams and Van Dorn 1999). In fact, the U.S. Surgeon General (2001) recently identified community disorganization as a small predictor of later violence for 14- to 16-year-olds.

A growing body of research suggests that children become witnesses, victims, or perpetrators of community violence, and the consequences of these violent episodes are negatively affecting their lives. Witnessing acts of interpersonal violence during childhood discourages some adolescents from engaging in normal community activities (Jenson and Howard 1999). Others perpetrate violent acts as they mature and grow into adulthood.

Americans are challenged by this dilemma and are faced with the need to develop ways of dealing with community violence. This chapter begins with discussion of research in community violence followed by a description of community violence prevention/intervention techniques. The interventions are based on the U.S. Surgeon General's (2001) recent report and it is assumed that Bronfenbrenner's (1979) and Noddings's (1984) theories undergird each intervention proposed.

VIOLENCE IN OUR COMMUNITIES

The type and amount of research conducted on community violence varies. For example, scant research exists on the relationship of children's exposure to community violence whereas a plethora of research has been conducted on community characteristics and its relationship to violence. Following is a general overview of the findings from various types of research on community violence.

Many children in the United States grow up in communities where violence—murders, assaults, random acts of violence, drive-by shootings, and gang activities—is a common occurrence. Mazza and Reynolds (1999) found that 93 percent of their participants who were inner-city adolescents attending a school in a low-income neighborhood in Brooklyn were exposed to at least one violent act in the community. Horn and Trickett (2001) and Veenema (2001) conducted a systematic literature review on the relationship of children's exposure to community violence (see Horn and Trickett and Veenema for review). Exposure to community violence has been defined as frequent and continual exposure to guns, knives, and drugs. Some of the studies reviewed by Horn and Trickett and Veenema reported that 80 percent to 90 percent of children living in urban settings are direct victims of or witnesses to significant acts of violence in their neighborhoods or communities (Fitzpatrick and Boldizar 1993; Jenkins and Bell 1997; Osofsky et al. 1993; Richters and Martinez 1993). This type of violence is not limited to adolescents. For example, Richters and Martinez, who conducted a study of 165 early elementary children from low-income neighborhoods in Washington, D.C., reported that 61 percent of 1st- and 2nd-grade students and 72 percent of 5th- and 6th-grade students had witnessed some type of community violence. In sum, these studies, although limited, suggest that exposure to community violence is related to significant stress and depression in children.

Other researchers have studied the relationship between violence and community characteristics, such as low socioeconomic status, poverty, and gangs. According to Limber and Nation (2001) "a substantial body of research over the past 40 years has established links between violent crime and poverty and related phenomena such as low socioeconomic status and unemployment" (175). In urban areas, the combination of poverty with instability and family disruption is predictive of violence (Bursik and

Grasmick 1993; Elliot, Wilson, et al. 1996). Research has also shown that communities with high levels of poverty have high rates of gang activity, a predictor for later violence of serious delinquent behavior. According to Spergel (1990), gang members commit the majority of serious youth violence. The U.S. Surgeon General (2001) reported that a high proportion of gang members are also involved in drug sales and possession of a gun, two behaviors closely linked to serious violent behaviors. It is estimated that 46 percent of youth gang members are involved in street drug sales (Egley 2000). In a longitudinal study conducted in Rochester, 67 percent of gang youths reported owning or carrying a gun for protection and 32 percent reported selling drugs (Thornberry 1998). Some gang activity takes place in schools, which increases the chance of students becoming victims of violence. The rate of victimization in schools having gangs is 7.5 percent, compared with 2.7 percent in schools without gangs. According to Snyder and Sickmund (1999) the chances of becoming a victim of violence are more than 2 1/2 times as great in schools where gangs are reported, and these schools are disproportionately located in disadvantaged, disorganized neighborhoods. Gangs in schools increased dramatically (by 15 percent to 28 percent) between 1989 and 1995 but have recently declined to 17 percent in 1999. Recent research suggests that students join gangs to strengthen their sense of belonging, their independence from parents, and their self-esteem (Hill et al. 1999).

Even if students are not gang members, research suggests that students who establish a relationship with delinquent peers are at high risk of becoming violent. Peer groups function in both neighborhoods and in schools, but the concentration of peer groups in schools may intensify the negative influence of these groups. Felson et al. (1994) conducted a study of adolescent males and found that some schools have dominant peer groups that value academic achievement and disapprove of violence, while others have groups that approve of the use of violence. This study found that the risk of becoming involved in violence varied depending on the dominant peer culture in their school, regardless of students' own views about the use of violence.

Social disorganization is a theoretical construct posed by researchers when studying the relationship between community characteristics and violence. Social disorganization and the presence of crime and drugs in the neighborhood has been identified as a risk for violence (U.S. Surgeon

General 2001). Furthermore, socially disorganized communities characterized by economic fluctuation, high turnover of residents, and a large
proportion of disrupted or single-parent families are predictive of more
delinquent activities and violent acts committed by youths who grow up
there. In these situations, it is less likely that there will be adult supervision of adolescent activities, providing an opportunity for high crime to
occur. In fact, the Office of Juvenile Justice and Delinquency Prevention
(1999a) conducted a study and found that most juvenile crimes occur immediately after school hours. It was also found that this is the same time
of day that children are more likely to become victims of crime. It appears
that schools located in disorganized neighborhoods are more likely to
have a high rate of violence than schools in other neighborhoods (Laub
and Lauritsen 1998). Moreover, areas where there is economic decline are
less likely to have neighborhood businesses and fewer opportunities for
children to be engaged in after-school activities or successful part-time
employment.

Social disorganization is not limited to certain areas or boundaries.
Rural areas are also experiencing social disorganization. Osgood and
Chambers (2000) found that rural areas experiencing residential instability, broken homes, and other indicators of social disorganization were at
greater risk for violence. At the same time it should be emphasized that
most of the violence to which young people are exposed takes place in
their home neighborhood or the neighborhood surrounding the school, not
in the school itself (Laub and Lauritsen 1998).

Individual schools, like individual students, do not necessarily reflect
the characteristics of the surrounding neighborhood. A stable, well-
administered school in a violent neighborhood may function as a safe
haven for students. In sum, research that focused on community characteristics and violence found that adolescents living in socially disorganized communities belonging to a gang or engaging in delinquent
relationships were at risk for violence. Therefore, it is important to identify community prevention and intervention strategies that could be used
to help reduce community violence. The following section describes possible prevention and intervention community strategies which are based
on the U.S. Surgeon General's (2001) report. In 1999, the Office of Juvenile Justice and Delinquency Prevention (OJJDP) studied family,
school, and community interventions used to prevent serious and juvenile

offenses. According to OJJDP (1999b), implementing effective interventions requires involvement from the family, school, and community. The intervention/prevention strategies posed here support that notion.

Community-Based Programs

Being aware of the risk factors, such as community disorganization and gangs, related to community violence is helpful when considering appropriate interventions/prevention strategies. To that end, the community intervention/prevention strategies presented appear to be the most effective when targeting several risk factors in a variety of settings. The U.S. Surgeon General (2001) discussed two intervention/prevention strategies, after-school programs and comprehensive community interventions, as possible ways to reduce violence. Research has shown that children/adolescents in socially disorganized neighborhoods may not have access to after-school activities. The U.S. Surgeon General reported that positive youth development programs are one way to help address this problem. Positive youth development programs are similar to the Big Boys and Girls Clubs and Big Brothers and Big Sisters of America programs. Research suggests that these types of programs have reduced vandalism, drug trafficking, and youth crime. Another program, the Canadian after-school program, was evaluated and found to have a positive effect on reducing violence. This after-school program provided supervised recreation after school. Its focus was to help reduce the alienation and association with delinquent or violent peers and introduce several ways to become involved in prosocial youth and adults in Ontario, Canada. This program actively recruited children ages 5 to 15 from low-income families who lived in Ontario public housing. Students participated in structured after-school courses designed to improve their sports and music, dance, scouting, and other non-athletic activities. According to the U.S. Surgeon General (2001) and the OJJDP (1999a) the number of arrests for juveniles participating in this after-school program was significantly lower than the number of arrests for the same number of juveniles two years before the intervention and for the same number of juveniles in the same housing project. Unfortunately, when the program was discontinued, the positive changes in the neighborhood diminished significantly, supporting the need to implement effective interventions that involve the family, school, and community continuously.

Comprehensive community interventions that hold promise for reducing youth violence and risk factors for youth violence are skills-oriented programs, such as the Midwestern Prevention Project. This project was designed to prevent substance abuse in forty-two public middle schools (grades 6 or 7) in the Kansas and Missouri area. The project had five components that were implemented consecutively during a four-year period: mass media program, school program, parent education, community organization, and local health policy to support the goals of the intervention. The mass media program occurred throughout the duration of the program, while the other components were introduced in approximately one-year spans. This project demonstrated positive effects on a number of levels that are closely tied to youth violence. For example, this project reduced smoking and marijuana use and lessened drug use through age 23. In addition, the project facilitated improvements in parent–child communication about drug use as well as the development of prevention programs, activities, and services in the community.

Although the Class of 1989 study is not cited in the U.S. Surgeon General's report, the success and findings of this study are similar to the Midwestern Prevention Project. The purpose of the Class of 1989 study was to prevent adolescent smoking and alcohol use. This study was part of the Minnesota Heart to Health Program (MHHP) conducted between 1980 and 1993. Part of the evaluation process examined the effect of a classroom-based smoking prevention curriculum implemented during the 1989 academic school year to 6th-, 7th-, and 8th-grade students and the communitywide heart health activities of MHHP. The results showed that students participating in this program smoked less compared with the control group. These results suggest that combined school and community interventions can help prevent drug use in middle school students.

Another program highlighted by the U.S. Surgeon General's report is the Yale Child Welfare Project. This thirty-month program uses in-home visitation and day care to conduct parent training and other child services. This intervention focuses on healthy, first-born infants from mothers who live in inner cities and have incomes below poverty level. Weekly home visits included securing visits from a social worker, pediatric medical care, psychological services, and early education for children. Another program focuses on older at-risk youths, ages 11 to 13, who live in disorganized neighborhoods: Striving Together to Achieve Rewarding Tomorrows (formally known as Children At Risk). This program has eight core components: (a) community-enhanced policing, (b) case management for youth and families, (c) criminal justice intervention, (d) family services, (e) after-school and summer activities, (f) educational services, (g) mentoring, and (h) incentives for participation. Research has shown that this program demonstrated positive effects on avoidance of drug use, violent crime, and drug sales. Moreover, these effects were maintained for up to one year after program participation.

Whereas the research presented here demonstrates that a large number of approaches and programs can have significant, positive effects on youth violence and violence-related risk factors, several popular prevention approaches used in high-risk populations have been shown to be ineffective. These include gun buy-back programs, firearm training, and mandatory gun ownership (U.S. Surgeon General 2001). Gun buy-back programs, a particularly expensive strategy, have consistently been shown to have no effect on gun violence, including firearm-related homicide and injury. These findings may seem conflicting given the fact that the gun buy-back programs remove guns from the street. However, there is some evidence that most of the guns turned in are not functional and that most persons turning in guns have other guns at home. Firearm training and mandatory gun ownership are two interventions that have also demonstrated no significant effects on firearm-related crimes. These approaches were expected to deter gun violence by increasing the number of private citizens who were trained to use guns properly and who owned firearms for protection.

Two additional community-based strategies for preventing youth violence—redirecting youth behavior and shifting peer group norms— have also shown a lack of effect in reducing youth violence. In fact, because both approaches tend to group high-risk youths together, they can actually increase the cohesiveness of delinquent peer groups and facilitate deviancy training (Dishion, Patterson, and Griesler 1994; Elliott and Menard 1996; Patterson and Yoerger 1997). Programs that aim to redirect high-risk youth toward conventional activities involve recreational, enrichment, and leisure activities, including the popular midnight basketball program. In general, programs that focus on shifting peer group norms have attempted to turn youth gangs into benign clubs. Instead, these programs have had no effect or have actually increased gang-related delinquent behavior.

CONCLUSION

Drawing on the works of Noddings (1984) and Bronfenbrenner (1979), the intervention/prevention strategies identified by the U.S. Surgeon General as effectively reducing violence at the macrosystem level, or the community level, rely heavily on the involvement of several microsystems, more specifically the school and family. This implies that interventions/prevention techniques directed toward single sources of influence are most likely to be unsuccessful. Instead, to be effective, programs must target several risk factors in a variety of settings. For example, the after-school programs not only help children in disorganized neighborhoods engage in positive learning activities, but they also help parents who may need to work and cannot financially afford a baby-sitter. As the African proverb states, "It takes a village to raise a child."

REFERENCES

Bronfenbrenner, U. 1979. *The ecology of human development: Experiments in nature and design*. Cambridge, Mass.: Harvard University Press.

Bursik, R. J., Jr., and H. G. Grasmick. 1993. *Neighborhoods and crime: The dimensions of effective community control*. New York: Lexington Books.

Dishion, T. J., G. R. Patterson, and P. C. Griesler. 1994. Peer adaptation in the development of antisocial behavior: A confluence model. In *Aggressive behavior: Current perspectives,* ed. L. R. Huesmann. New York: Plenum.

Egley, A., Jr. 2000. *Highlights of the 1999 National Youth Gang Survey* (Fact Sheet 20). Washington, D.C.: Office of Juvenile Justice and Delinquency Prevention.

Elliot, D. S., and S. Menard. 1996. Delinquent friends and delinquent behaviors: Temporal and developmental patterns. In *Current theories of crime and deviance,* ed. J. D. Hawkins. Thousand Oaks, Calif.: Sage.

Elliott, D. S., W. J. Wilson, D. Huizinga, A. C. Elliott, and B. Ranking. 1996. The effects of neighborhood disadvantage on youth development. *Journal of Research in Crime and Delinquency* 33: 389–426.

Felson, R., A. Liska, S. South, and T. McNulty. 1994. The subculture of violence and delinquency: Individual vs. school context effects. *Social Forces* 73: 155–73.

Fitzpatrick, K. M., and J. P. Boldizar. 1993. The prevalence and consequences of exposure to violence among African-American youth. *Journal of American Academy of Child and Adolescent Psychiatry* 32: 424–30.

Hill, K. G., J. C. Howell, J. D. Hawkins, and S. R. Battin-Pearson. 1999. Childhood risk factors for adolescent gang membership: Results form the Seattle Social Development Project. *Journal of Research in Crime and Delinquency* 36: 300–22.

Horn, J. L., and P. K. Trickett. 2001. Community violence and child development: A review of research. In *Constructive and destructive behavior implications for family, school, and society,* ed. A. C. Bohart and D. J. Stipek, pp. 103–38. Washington, D.C.: American Psychological Association.

Jenkins, E. J., and C. C. Bell. 1997. Exposure and response to community violence among children and adolescents. In *Children in a violent society,* ed. J. D. Osofsky. New York: Guilford Press.

Jenson, J. M., and M. O. Howard. 1999. Cause of youth violence. In *Youth violence: Current research and recent practice innovations,* ed. J. M. Jenson and M. O. Howard. Washington, D.C.: NASW Press.

Laub, J. H., and J. L. Lauritsen. 1998. The interdependence of school violence with neighborhood and family conditions. In *Violence in American schools: A new perspective,* ed. D. S. Elliott, B. A. Hamburg, and K. R. Williams. New York: Cambridge University Press.

Limber, S. P., and M. A. Nation. 2001. Violence within the neighborhood and community. In *Constructive and destructive behavior implications for family, school, and society,* ed. A. C. Bohart and D. J. Stipek, pp. 171–93. Washington, D.C.: American Psychological Association.

Mazza, J. J., and W. M. Reynolds. 1999, June. Exposure to violence in inner-city adolescents: Relationships of suicidal ideation, depression, and PTSD symptomatology. *Journal of Abnormal Child Psychology* 27: 203–13.

Noddings, N. 1984. *Caring: A feminine approach to ethics and moral education.* Berkeley: University of California Press.

Office of Juvenile Justice and Delinquency Prevention. 1999a. *Violence after school.* Washington, D.C.: Author.

Office of Juvenile Justice and Delinquency Prevention. 1999b. *School and community interventions to prevent serious and violent offending.* Washington, D.C.: Author.

Osgood, D. W., and J. M. Chambers. 2000. Social disorganization outside metropolis: An analysis of rural youth violence. *Criminology* 38: 81–111.

Osofsky, J. D., S. Wewers, D. M. Hann, and A. C. Fick. 1993. Chronic community violence: What is happening to our children? *Psychiatry* 56: 36–45.

Patterson, G. R., and K. Yoerger. 1997. A development model for late-onset delinquency. In *Motivation and delinquency,* ed. D. W. Osgood. Lincoln: University of Nebraska Press.

Richters, J. E., and P. E. Martinez. 1993. The NIMH community violence project: I. Children as victims of witnesses to violence. *Psychiatry* 56: 7–21.

Snyder, H., and M. Sickmund. 1999. *Juvenile offenders and victims: 1999 national report* (NCJ 17825). Washington, D.C.: Office of Juvenile Justice and Delinquency Prevention, at www.ncjrs.org/html/ojjdp/national report99/toc. html (accessed February 22, 2001).

Spergel, I. A. 1990. Youth gangs: Continuity and change. In *Youth violence. Crime and justice: A review of the research,* ed. M. Tonry and N. Morris. Chicago: University of Chicago Press.

Thornberry, T. P. 1998. Membership in youth gangs and involvement in serious violent offending. In *Serious and violent juvenile offenders: Risk factors and successful interventions,* ed. R. Loeber and D. P. Farrington. Thousand Oaks, Calif.: Sage.

U.S. Surgeon General. 2001. *Youth violence: A report of the surgeon general.* Washington, D.C.: U.S. Surgeon General's Office, at http://surgeongeneral.gov. library/youthviolence/toc.html (accessed February 22, 2002).

Veenema, T. 2001. Children's exposure to community violence. *Journal of Nursing Scholarship* 33(2): 167–73.

Williams, J. H., and R. A. Van Dorn. 1999. Delinquency, gangs, and youth violence. In *Youth violence: Current research and recent practice innovations,* ed. J. M. Jenson and M. O. Howard. Washington, D.C.: NASW Press.

Index

About the Contributors

Denise Smith is an assistant professor at Indiana University at South Bend, in the department of special education. Before receiving her doctorate from the University of South Florida, she worked as a special education teacher for children with mild disabilities. Her research interests include teacher reflection and school violence. She has recently co-authored a chapter on school violence and its effect on children with special needs.

Karen B. Clark is program coordinator and assistant professor of special education at Indiana University South. She received her Ph.D. in special education from Penn State University. She currently teaches undergraduate and graduate methods and foundational classes. Her research interests include the redesign of teacher education programs and teacher efficacy. She recently received Indiana's Distinguished Teacher Educator Award from the Indiana Association of Colleges for Teacher Education.

James Hurst is an assistant professor of counseling and human services at Indiana University, South Bend. He recieved his Ph.D. in clinical and health pyschology from the University of Florida and is licensed as a health service provider in psychology in Indiana. He has extensive clinical experience working with adolescents, adults, couples, and families. He currently teaches graduate courses in consulting theory, group process, and psychopathology. His research interests include youth substance abuse prevention and targeted school violence.

John King is in the master's degree program in counseling and human services at Indiana University at South Bend. He holds a bachelor's degree in music education from Butler University and a master's degree in music education from DePaul University in Chicago. He has been teaching at the secondary level for seventeen years and is currently teaching in the Northwestern School Corporation in Kokomo, Indiana. His research interests include school counseling, youth/school violence, and developing student leadership.

Patricia A. Parrish is an assistant professor of education and coordinator of internships at Saint Leo University, where she teaches coursework in special education and elementary education. Her research interests include caring in the student–teacher relationship and values-infused education. She has published and presented at national conferences on the topics of caring and the education of those with cognitive disabilities.